Mental Health Matters
in Primary Care

Mental Health Matters
in Primary Care

Elaine Millar and Mark Walsh

Stanley Thornes (Publishers) Ltd

First published in 2000 by:
Stanley Thornes (Publishers) Ltd
Ellenborough House
Wellington Street
Cheltenham
Glos.
GL50 1YW
United Kingdom

00 01 02 03 / 10 9 8 7 6 5 4 3 2 1

A catalogue record for this book is available from the British Library

ISBN 0 7487 4528 9

Typeset by Gray Publishing, Tunbridge Wells, Kent
Printed and bound in Great Britain by Martins the Printers, Berwick upon Tweed

Contents

PREFACE

This book came about because of a research project that looked at the care of people with schizophrenia who receive their regular depot anti-psychotic from a practice nurse. It became clear that most of these referrals were made to a nurse because there was an injection to be given. This was always seen as a nursing duty. However, the nurses, aware of the broader implications of this role, expressed concern; most of them had little or no psychiatric training or experience. They welcomed information and support in caring for this patient group and they asked if there was a book . . .

Mental Health Matters in Primary Care is written specifically for primary health care nurses. It is for practice nurses, district nurses, health visitors, occupational health nurses, accident and emergency and school nurses. They are on the front line – often the first to suspect and identify mental health problems – and they remain pivotal throughout, sustaining many people with mental health problems in the community.

This is both an instant guidebook for 'in-the-field' and 'on-the-job' situations and a handbook for planning and implementing individual patient care and developing practice protocols. It is also a comprehensive reference book for individual and group study, useful to general student nurses, as well as those on post-registration community courses. Indeed, it will provide a valuable resource for workers in other related professions, such as social work, the police and courts and residential and nursing homes.

The book is divided into three sections. The first section serves to introduce or re-familiarize the reader (practitioner) with mental health issues: it explains the basic terms used and provides a helpful justification for its emphasis on the 'medical model' approach to care. The second section comprehensively covers a range of mental disorders and mental health issues. For each, the questions 'What is it?', 'What causes it?', 'Who does it affect?' and 'What can be done?' are addressed. Highlighted 'key points' boxes present the information in a concise and easily accessible way. The case studies aim to breathe life into the factual information and to provide valuable management guidelines. Section three builds on the previous section by addressing the key resource issues facing primary health care workers. Included are an extensive, alphabetical list of resources, information about anti-psychotic medication and a glossary of key terms and conditions. There is an emphasis on patient assessment and review running throughout the book and a unique feature, also to be found in the final section, is a collection of assessment tools – developed for non-specialists and intended to be photocopied from the book for the nurse to use with individual patients. The aim of the resource section is to provide relevant information in a way that is practically applicable in a primary care setting.

The brief of the primary health care nurse is as broad and varied as the health and welfare needs of each of us. This book aims to inform, support and empower them as they deal with our mental health matters.

ACKNOWLEDGEMENTS

Elaine Millar: I would like to thank Professor Tom Burns and the 'research team' at St George's Hospital Medical School, London, and especially the practice nurses who were the kick-start for this book. Thanks also to Linda Cooke and Patricia Fraser for careful proof-reading and helpful comments, and to Carol Wannan for her valuable comments on the content. Thanks and love always to Russell, to both our supportive families, and to our steadfast friends – especially for entertaining Jim, Alasdair and Robbie long enough for me to write the book.

Mark Walsh: I would like to thank my friends, present and former colleagues and my family for their ideas, advice and support. Special thanks and love to Karen for being fun and an inspiration.

The Publishers gratefully acknowledge the copyright holders for permission to use the following material: Figures 1.3.1 and 1.3.2 reproduced with permission from *OPCS Survey, Report 1*, Meltzer *et al.*, Office for National Statistics © Crown Copyright 1995. Figure 1.33 reproduced with the permission of BMJ Publishing Group, from *Clinical Review*, **314**, 1609, Craig and Boardman, 1997. Figure 2.31 reproduced with the permission of Macmillian Press Ltd from *Mental Health Issues in Primary Care – a practical guide*, Armstrong, 1995.

MENTAL HEALTH MATTERS IN PRIMARY CARE

During the 1980s half of all psychiatric in-patient beds in the UK were closed as part of the move to replace residential in-patient psychiatric care with care in the community. The policy of closing large, segregating psychiatric hospitals and delivering care in the community, with varying degrees of support and supervision, is just one of the factors that have brought mental health and illness issues to the attention of primary health care professionals. Recent government policy has also given primary health care practitioners a specific role in providing services that meet the mental health care needs of the general population, as well as contributing to the ongoing community care of people with severe and enduring mental illnesses. In some ways this is not new. Much of the 'mental morbidity' experienced by the general population has always been dealt with in primary health care, rather than in specialist psychiatric settings. For most people who experience mild symptoms of mental distress, their GP practice has always been the first port of call.

Primary health care professionals have become increasingly involved in the diagnosis and treatment of mental illness as part of their everyday work over the last decade. In addition to the above factors this is the result of:

- a new policy focus on a primary care-led NHS
- the identification of mental illness as a key health improvement area with national reduction targets
- a growing awareness of the relatively high levels of preventable and treatable 'mental morbidity' in the general population.

Therefore, this book has been written to provide primary health care professionals with a focused, accessible source of reference and support material on mental health matters. It is particularly aimed at practice nurses and other general-trained nurses who wish to develop a greater awareness, knowledge and understanding of the mental health and illness matters with which they are required to deal on a regular basis.

1.1 PROFESSIONS, PERSPECTIVES AND PSYCHIATRY

Mental health and illness can be conceptualized and referred to in different ways. The following list of terms can all be used to indicate that a person is experiencing some sort of disorder or difficulty in relation to their feelings, behaviour and/or mental experiences:

- Mental health problems
- Mental illness
- Mental distress
- Mental disorder

- Madness
- Psychological problems
- Psychiatric problems.

The plethora of definitions and ways of referring to mental health and illness occur because this area is heavily 'contested' by professional and service user groups who compete to apply differing explanations (medical, social, cognitive, psychoanalytical and behavioural) and intervention approaches to the mental morbidity that people experience. While accepting that there are many ways of describing and explaining mental morbidity, the book is fundamentally concerned with helping you to identify and respond to the mental distress that people experience and present in the primary care setting.

Some of the terms used above are more socially and professionally acceptable than others. Few mental health professionals will use the term 'madness' to describe mental morbidity, though there are also a significant proportion who, in using a social model, reject the 'illness' idea. The different models of mental disorder tend to have their own specific terminology and may give slightly different meanings to terms that are similar or the same. An awareness of the various ways of describing and defining aspects of mental morbidity and its treatment is helpful (see 'Glossary', p. 157), given that most health care is now provided through multidisciplinary team approaches.

While various models of mental disorder inform the problem-framing and intervention approaches of professionals in different ways, the dominant language used to describe and define mental morbidity is that of psychiatry. It is by far the most commonly used approach in statutory and private sector mental health services and also fits into the general medical model that primary health care professionals tend to work with. Psychiatry is a branch of medicine dealing with disorders in which mental or behavioural features are most prominent (Davies, 1997).

We outline in 'psychiatric' terms the key 'mental' conditions that people tend to present with in primary health care settings throughout the book. In doing so we are describing the ways in which people's feelings, thoughts and behaviour become disordered so that they experience distress and problems with their normal functioning. We believe that primary health care professionals who are not mental health specialists will find this approach the most useful one. We are not suggesting that this is the only valid way of describing or understanding mental morbidity or that it is necessarily the most appropriate in other settings.

1.2 COMING TO TERMS WITH MENTAL ILLNESS

In using a medical psychiatry approach to our descriptions of mental morbidity we are accepting the idea of mental illness. Most people are aware of the concept of mental illness but prefer not to think too much about it. Mental illness is a stigmatized term. It conjures up images, ideas and feelings that people fear, and people avoid what they fear. This can be a problem for people who develop mental illnesses and for professionals who work with them. Many commonly held ideas about mental illness are inaccurate and are informed by prejudice. Myths and stereotypes about mental illnesses, and the people who experience them, are still common. The 'lunatic', 'madman' and 'nutter' labels that regularly feature in tabloid headlines perpetuate the stigma that is attached to mental illness. Violence and danger are commonly seen to be a part of the 'mentally ill' person's make-up.

The impression given by newspaper and media coverage is that in pre-community care days the population of Britain used to relax more comfortably in their beds at night. It is suggested that they felt, and were, more secure in the knowledge that the 'mentally ill' were safely segregated in hospitals that cut them off and kept them away from the 'mentally healthy' majority of the population. The media frequently paints a 'them' and 'us' picture, in which the 'mentally ill' are not like 'us' and that we're better off keeping clear of 'them'.

But the situation is no longer like that, if indeed it ever was. As newspapers and television programmes have regularly pointed out over the past 10 years, the policy of 'care in the community' has largely ended the segregation and incarceration of people experiencing mental illness. The care in the community policy was partly driven by a change in attitude towards, and thinking about, mental health and illness but also recognized that most people experiencing mental ill-health never experienced a hospital admission anyway.

It is now unhelpful and inappropriate to think of there being a distinct, identifiable, separate group of 'mentally ill' people. All sorts of people, for various reasons and at various points in their lives, experience mental illness. Coming to terms with mental illness, for non-specialist primary care professionals involves accepting that people, at certain times in their lives, experience forms of mental morbidity that cause them distress and disruption but which are generally of a temporary nature. In many ways it is important to normalize mental illness.

Normalizing mental illness – a continuum of mental health and illness?

Imagine that you are an average 'mentally healthy' individual. If you were to look closely into your mind and became as familiar with it as you are with your body, you would probably accept, though you might not care to admit it, that people who experience mental illness are not so different to you. We all have moments, perhaps even days or months, of fear, anxiety, depression, anger, and suspicion. Many of us will also have experienced life crises, or problems in living, which have disturbed our social and psychological equilibrium and perhaps even made us physically unwell at times. Life has probably had its 'ups and downs' for most of us and may have affected our relationships, social functioning and work performance as a result. But we're not mentally ill, are we? Perhaps your mental distress wasn't recognized as 'illness', either by yourself or others. The dividing line between being mentally healthy and having an experience of mental illness is hard to define and to recognize. Do you know how much stress is too much for you? What sets of circumstances could lead you to cross the indistinct health–illness divide, if it is a 'divide' at all? Our social and psychological functioning and 'well-being' is not a constant thing. It fluctuates – we move up and down a mental health/ill-health continuum all the time. Extreme fluctuations, or persistent experiences that impair our capacity to cope with everyday living, may result in an experience that can be described as mental illness. As the prevalence statistics on p. 7 suggest, it is really not so unusual to experience a degree of mental illness at some point in life. Given the prevalence of mental morbidity in the general population and the fact that most symptoms are more extreme experiences of common feelings, behaviours and thought patterns, mental illness is far more 'normal' than most people realize.

Describing and identifying mental illness

It is not possible to draw up a simple list of symptoms or do a test that will tell you definitively whether someone is or isn't mentally ill. People experience mental disorder and express mental distress in various ways (see Table 1.2.1).

Most lay people would identify extreme mental illness as some fearful form of unsightly, uncontrollable 'madness' and blissful happiness and contentment as evidence of mental health. In between these two hypothetical extremes, there is a vast range of emotional and psychological experience that is much harder to describe and 'classify' in health and illness terms. For example, look at the following patient 'presentations':

- a stressed, anxious mother of three children under 5 who complains of 'feeling inadequate and useless'
- a teenager who cannot sleep without taking a sedative tablet
- a teacher who is losing control over his alcohol consumption as a new term approaches

Table 1.2.1

How does mental disorder/distress show itself?

Emotionally
- Frequent changes of mood
- Persistent, unchanging mood
- Feeling very low or very elated
- Not feeling anything
- Unable to identify or empathize with feelings of others

Cognitively
- Poor concentration
- Confused/muddled thinking
- Interrupted thoughts
- Bizarre thoughts
- Repetitive, unwanted thoughts

Behaviourally
- Erratic and culturally inappropriate behaviour
- Agitation
- Withdrawal
- Aggression/violence to others
- Self-harm

Physiologically
- Poor/broken sleep
- Changes in appetite/weight change
- Changes in energy levels
- Loss of sexual interest/energy
- Physical tension
- Unexplained headaches

- a truanting and 'glue-sniffing' school child who is out of her parents' control
- a newly married woman who is fearful of sex but unable to tell her husband
- an older woman with a failing memory and ability to concentrate
- a man who regularly visits his GP with vague symptoms and minor complaints that have no apparent physical causes
- a business woman who experiences incapacitating headaches when faced by extra pressure at work.

Are any or all of these people mentally ill? Each person seems to have problems with living, coping and establishing a sense of psychological and emotional 'well-being'. While they may share many of the characteristics and experiences of the 'mentally healthy', their problems, and the distress they experience as a result of them, differentiate them both from their 'normal self' and from other, mentally healthy, people. This comparison with their 'normal self' and others is important in identifying mental illness. It may well be that each of these individuals is experiencing some 'mental ill-health' at this point in their life. However, in order to establish a clinical diagnosis you would need to be aware of and identify a particular, characteristic pattern of clinical signs and symptoms.

Identifying psychiatric illness

Methods of identifying and assessing psychiatric problems in primary care are discussed in detail in Chapter 3.1. At this point we will outline how different patterns of signs and symptoms are grouped together into diagnostic categories that are commonly used by primary care professionals working with people who present with apparent mental morbidity.

'Diseases' are diagnosed by reference to observable, objective physical pathology. There are very few identifiable psychiatric diseases, though advances in behavioural genetics and neuro-imaging techniques may change this. Psychiatric illnesses are identified through the subjective distress that people report and also through the identification of patterns of symptoms that characterize and define specific disorders.

Psychiatric illnesses are classified according to their similarities in symptoms, the course and prognosis of the illness, and their response to treatment. There are a number of ways of classifying the spectrum of mental illnesses. These include categorical systems in which a hierarchy of separate conditions is defined and individuals are given a main diagnosis. The more commonly used multi-axial systems, such as the International Classification of Disease (ICD) approach, categorize the person's symptoms on several axes and rely on specified criteria, such as the number of symptoms and the length of time they should be present, rather than descriptive definitions. In this book we use descriptive definitions.

Primary health care professionals who are not mental health specialists or medical practitioners are not likely to have the time, training or inclination to carry out a formal diagnostic assessment of a patient's symptoms in order to arrive at an ICD diagnosis. It is probably more useful to be able to recognize patterns of symptoms from observation and the individual's brief, and possibly informal, self-report. Subsequent chapters describe the presenting signs and symptoms of:

- schizophrenia
- bipolar affective disorder
- depression
- anxiety disorders
- substance misuse and addictions
- deliberate self-harm and suicide
- eating disorders
- dementia
- life stresses and adjustment.

The mental health problems described in the book are those that are relatively common, or prevalent, in the population, such as depressive disorder and those less common illnesses, such as schizophrenia, with which primary health care professionals increasingly come into contact.

1.3 MENTAL MORBIDITY IN THE UK POPULATION

Epidemiological data on the prevalence of psychiatric morbidity in the population of the UK reveal how commonly symptoms of mental ill-health are experienced and give some insight into the differing patterns of prevalence between different groups in the population.

About one in six adults (aged 16–64 years old) surveyed by the OPCS (Meltzer *et al.*, 1995) suffered from a neurotic disorder. This was most likely to be a mixed anxiety and depressive disorder (77 cases per 1000). Generalized anxiety was prevalent in 31 cases per 1000. Other neurotic disorders, such as obsessive compulsive disorder and phobias are less prevalent. Women are more likely to experience neurotic disorders than men.

Psychoses, such as schizophrenia and bipolar disorder, have a much lower prevalence than neurotic disorders. The prevalence rate is about 4 per 1000 with little difference between men and women. However, substance misuse and addiction is more likely in men than women. Men are three times more likely to have an alcohol dependence than women and are twice as likely to be drug dependent.

The graphs below describe the relative prevalence of various kinds of mental morbidity by sex (Figures 1.3.1 and 1.3.2).

More detail on the incidence and distribution of the disorders covered in the book is provided in respective subsequent chapters.

Diversity and mental health

The social and cultural diversity of the population of the UK is a factor that primary care professionals ought to take into account when trying to understand patterns and presentations of mental morbidity. The

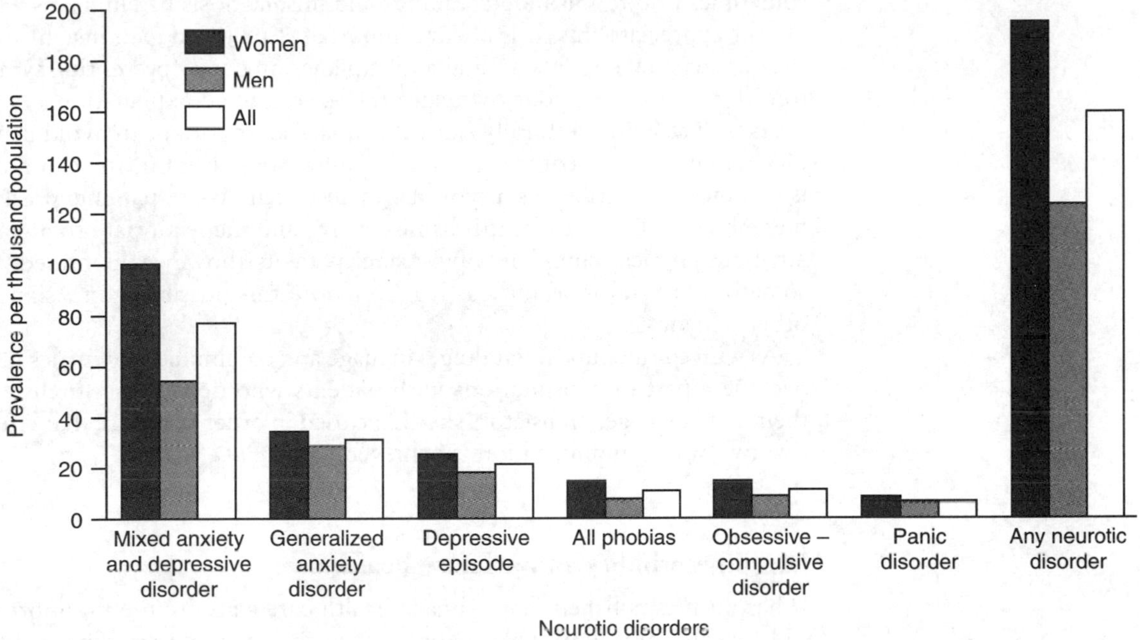

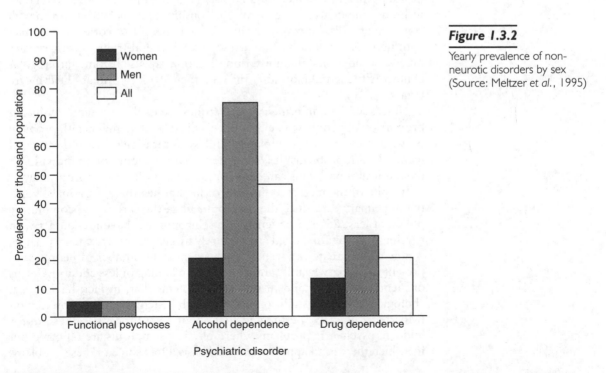

Figure 1.3.1

Weekly prevalence of neurotic disorders by sex (Source: Meltzer et al., 1995)

Figure 1.3.2

Yearly prevalence of non-neurotic disorders by sex (Source: Meltzer et al., 1995)

presentation of mental health problems and help-seeking behaviour is influenced by social factors such as culture and gender.

An individual's view of what being 'ill' involves and what experiences count as 'symptoms' of mental illness is culturally determined. This can sometimes lead to misunderstandings and misdiagnosis by clinicians who do not appreciate this. It is always important to try and gain insight into the patient's own understanding and explanation of any presenting symptoms before offering your own culturally-determined explanation.

As well as being culturally sensitive, it is also important to avoid using blanket cultural stereotypes inappropriately. Somatization, for example, is commonly described as a typical way in which 'Asian' patients present mental morbidity. Clearly, it is as insensitive and inappropriate to always attribute physical complaints by 'Asian' patients (however identified) to somatized mental morbidity as it is to ignore this possibility in Asian or other patient groups.

As with cultural understanding, language and communication issues may become a part of consultations with patients who do not use English as their first language. Translators should be used in order to ensure that effective two-way communication is achieved.

Mental morbidity and primary health care

It has been established that primary health care staff are the first port of call for, and deal with, most people when they are experiencing mental health problems. Goldberg and Huxley (1992) estimate that between one-fifth and one-quarter of general GP consultations have a mental health component. GPs, however, are not the only people to come into contact with users of primary health care services. General-trained primary care nurses, occupational therapists and physiotherapists all come into regular contact with mental morbidity through their work in primary health care teams.

Nurses working in primary care settings are likely to meet a significant proportion of people who either have a diagnosed mental health problem or who present with complaints and symptoms that are indicative of mental health problems. It is important that the nature of an individual's mental health problems can be identified and dealt with appropriately.

In spite of the increased number of mental health professionals working in primary care since the development of the care in the community policy, at least 25% of patients with schizophrenia have no contact with psychiatrists but are looked after entirely by general practice teams. There is now also a greater awareness of the significant number of people who present to primary health care services complaining of less enduring forms of mental morbidity and of physical problems that, in fact, have a psychological cause. A study published by the Mental Health Foundation (Morriss *et al.*, 1997) estimated that about 15% of visits to GPs are for 'hidden' psychiatric problems where physical symptoms are reported but for which there is no apparent physical basis. Only some of these problems

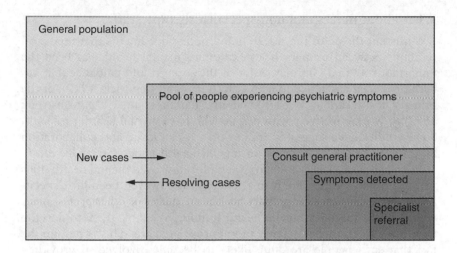

will be identified and fewer still will require a specialist referral (see Figure
1.3.3).

1.4 THE ROLE OF THE PRIMARY HEALTH CARE TEAM

Awareness, knowledge and understanding of mental illness presentations
and treatments in the primary health care setting are important for all
primary health care workers. In a report by the NHS Centre for Review
and Dissemination (*Effective Healthcare* 1997; 3: 3), primary health care
professionals are identified as playing a key role in identifying children
and adults who are vulnerable to mental health problems.

The report recommends that primary health care teams should be aware
of local services in order to refer people to appropriate sources of information and intervention in the statutory, voluntary and private sectors.

Characteristics of people at high risk of developing mental health problems (Source: Wise, 1997)

Adults who are:

- undergoing divorce or separation
- unemployed
- at risk of depression in pregnancy
- experiencing bereavement
- long-term carers of people who are highly dependent.

Children who are:

- living in poverty
- exhibiting behavioural difficulties
- experiencing parental separation and divorce
- within families experiencing bereavement.

What about nurses and non-specialist therapy staff?

A consistent theme of the research and policy documents that report on the links between primary health care and mental health has been the important role that GPs play. A lot of the support and guidance that has been produced has aimed to help GPs (Burns and Kendrick, 1997), or the primary health care team more generally (Jenkins *et al.*, 1992; Armstrong 1997) to work effectively with people who have mental health problems. Some studies have suggested frameworks for practice and collaboration by primary health care teams on mental health issues (Strathdee *et al.*, 1996; Gask *et al.*, 1997) and have called for improved mental health skills within primary health care teams. There has, however, been little specific support or guidance for primary health care nurses or other professionals who have no specialist mental health training to enable them to develop their skills or to offer effective and appropriate care. This is despite the fact that such people are quite likely to become involved in providing aspects of care to people who have significant mental health needs.

This book provides information and guidance on how to identify and manage the key features of common mental illnesses and provides some pointers to sources of help and support. A key theme of the book is that all people experience fluctuations in their mental state which at times, and for various reasons, can lead to an experience of mental ill-health. While for some people, this experience is a long-term, enduring one, for others it is a one-off, acutely experienced episode. Remember that a person who experiences mental ill-health is not a different kind of person, somehow separate and distinct from 'normal' society. Mental illness is an experience that any person can have, but which some seem more likely to have, for various reasons. Research suggests that primary health care professionals, especially nurses, are in a position to identify and help people experiencing such problems.

REFERENCES

Armstrong, E. (1997). *The Primary Mental Health Care Toolkit*. London: Department of Health and Royal College of General Practitioners, Unit for Mental Health Education in Primary Care.

Burns, T. and Kendrick, A. (1997). Guidelines on caring for people with serious mental illness in primary care. *British Journal of General Practice*, **47**, 515–520.

Craig, T.K.J. and Boardman, A.P. (1997). ABC of mental health: common mental health problems in primary care. *British Medical Journal*, **314**, 1609.

Davies, T. (1997). ABC of mental health: mental health assessment. *British Medical Journal*, **314**, 1536.

Gask, L. *et al.* (1997). Evaluating models of working at the interface between mental health services and primary care. *British Journal of Psychiatry*, **170**, 6–11.

Goldberg, D. and Huxley, P. (1992). *Common Mental Disorders: A Bio-social Model*. London: Routledge.

Jenkins, R., Newton and J., Young, R. (Eds.) (1992). *Prevention of Depression and Anxiety: The Role of the Primary Care Team*. London: HMSO.

Meltzer, H., Gill, B., Petticrew, M. and Hinds, K. (1995). *The Prevalence of Psychiatric Morbidity Among Adults Living in Private Households*, OPCS Surveys of Psychiatric Morbidity in Great Britain, Report 1. London: HMSO.

Morriss, R. *et al*. (1997). GP Management of 'Hidden' Psychiatric Problems, MHF Briefing No. 7. London: Mental Health Foundation.

Strathdee, G., Mead, N. and Gask, L. (1996). *A General Practitioner's Guide to Managing Long-term Mental Health Disorders*. London: The Sainsbury Centre for Mental Health.

Wise, J. (1997). Health professionals can prevent mental health problems. *British Medical Journal*, **315**, 327–332.

FURTHER READING

Bower, P., Mead, N. and Gask, L. (1997). Primary care and mental health problems. *Nursing Times*, **93**, 58–59.

Cohen, A. (1998). First port of call. *Open Mind*, **89**, 14–15.

Craig, T.K.J. and Boardman, A.P. (1997). ABC of mental health: common mental health problems in primary care. *British Medical Journal*, **314**, 1609.

Gale, C., Clinton, K. and Abboyi, M. (1997). Mind matters. *Nursing Times*, **93**, 36–37.

Warner, L. and Ford, R. (1998). Mental health facilitators in primary care. *Nursing Standard*, **13**, 36–40.

COMMON MENTAL DISORDERS

2

2.1 SCHIZOPHRENIA

There is no such thing as 'a schizophrenic' only a diverse range of people who suffer in many different ways from the illness of schizophrenia.

Roberts (1996)

Definition of schizophrenia

The word schizophrenia literally means 'split mind', which has given rise to the inaccurate description of the illness as a split personality, where the sufferer behaves in 'Jekyll and Hyde' fashion.

Schizophrenia is a severe psychotic mental illness marked by a distortion and fragmentation of the normal pathways between thinking, emotions, perceptions and behaviour. The course of the illness is episodic where, in an acute phase, symptoms of hallucinations, delusions, and thought disorder interfere with the sufferer's ability to make sense of the world and they are said to be out of touch with reality. However it is their reality; absolutely real to them. In the longer term this interferes with the ability to maintain relationships and function normally in society and leads to more chronic characteristics of social and emotional withdrawal and self-neglect.

Background

Schizophrenia has been a recognized diagnosis for over 150 years but the term was not used until 1911, when it was coined by Bleuler. Since then diagnosis has undergone refinements but there is no definitive diagnostic test. It can be described as a syndrome of symptoms, some of which are apparent in other psychiatric and organic conditions, and therefore consideration of differential diagnoses is vital. A number of classification systems have been developed to aid this process and hospital admission may be required to facilitate close observation of the patient over a period of time.

Prognosis

Schizophrenia can be viewed along a continuum of severity, where one-quarter of sufferers make a full early recovery, one-tenth become severely disabled, many requiring permanent residential or hospital care, and the remainder – the majority – suffer acute relapses at intervals and endure persisting symptoms. There is a significant incidence of suicide (estimated

Key points ➤

What is schizophrenia?
- It is not a 'split personality'.
- It is a psychotic mental disorder characterized in the acute stages by the sufferer losing touch with reality due to distorted thinking and perceptions.
- Longer-term, chronic characteristics of social and emotional withdrawal and self-neglect affect normal functioning in society.
- Diagnosis is reached through psychiatric assessment and observation: there is no definitive diagnostic test.
- Two-thirds suffer acute relapses and endure persisting symptoms.
- Ten per cent commit suicide; young men are most at risk.

at 10%), where young males are shown to be at most risk. While intelligence is not affected, the ability to think and reason is interfered with.

Signs and symptoms

The terms 'positive symptoms' and 'negative symptoms' are used to describe the whole picture of the illness (see Table 2.1.1). Patients will not necessarily exhibit all these symptoms.

Incidence and distribution

Schizophrenia is the most common, severe and enduring psychiatric illness and is found in most countries across the world, equally affecting males and females, and between 0.5% and 1% of the population. There is a higher incidence in urban areas – inner city GPs have an average of 12 patients on their list – probably explained by a drift towards cities following discharge from in-patient psychiatric care. Onset commonly occurs in adolescence and young adulthood, with another surge in the 30–45-year-old age group. There are no social class distinctions. In Britain a diagnosis of schizophrenia is more frequently made among young black men of Afro-Caribbean origin; whether this is explained by biology or the result of one culture's interpretation of another's norms, or, indeed, some other reason, is questionable.

An unfairly stigmatizing misconception is that people with schizophrenia are more likely to become violent. High profile cases, given great exposure in the media, have led to this inaccurate picture. However, statistics show that one is far more likely to be harmed by people in the general population and the greatest danger is of the sufferer harming himself or herself.

Positive symptoms (florid, psychotic, or first rank symptoms)	Negative symptoms
Hallucinations – false perceptions occurring without stimuli, that affect the five senses, commonly hearing, where voices are heard. May be one voice or many, which address the sufferer directly or talk about him or her, often in the form of a running commentary. May be experienced as emanating from inside or outside the head. May be persecutory in nature. Many sufferers continue to hear voices, even when treated, but are able to live with them and occasionally to build up a positive relationship with them.	*Social withdrawal* – perhaps unsurprising, given the onslaught of these immensely disruptive positive symptoms. As the illness reaches a more chronic stage, the withdrawal becomes more noticeable and health care workers, particularly those in primary care, often have to be pro-active in maintaining contact with patients.
Delusions – fixed and unshakeable false beliefs. May be singular or form systems that influence the patient's behaviour. They are often persecutory or grandiose in nature. The content usually holds some particular significance to the sufferer and therefore needs to be understood within the context of their cultural and social background.	*Blunted emotions* (also called 'affect') – manifested in an expressionless face and voice and a flattening of emotional responses. *Incongruous emotions* ('affect') – inappropriate expression of emotions, such as laughing at sad events.
Thought disorder – a variety of disruptions and distortions to the process of thinking. Examples include: *Thought insertion* – where an 'alien' thought is put into the sufferer's mind *Thought withdrawal* – where the opposite intrusion is believed to have occurred *Thought broadcast* – which describes the belief that others are privy to one's thoughts *Thought block* – apparent during conversation with the sufferer, where sudden cessation of speech indicates the blocking of thinking *Knight's move thinking* – jumping from one subject to another as the sufferer makes connections that are not apparent to listeners *Neologisms* – new words created by the sufferer or ordinary words used in an unusual way *Word salad* – a jumble of words *Clang association* – the phenomenon of a seemingly compulsory stringing together of similar sounding words.	*Inertia and apathy* – can cause the patient to spiral down into a life-style of self-neglect. *Clinical depression* – is commonly present, although often untreated, disguised as it is by the many other symptoms of schizophrenia. *Catatonic behaviour* – a fairly rare phenomenon since the introduction of anti-psychotic medication, where there is barely any physical activity and the sufferer will take up bizarre postures and maintain them for long periods of time, termed 'waxy flexibility'.
Ideas of reference – where apparently meaningless gestures or actions on the part of others, perhaps seen or said on TV, are imbued with special significance, which the sufferer believes everyone understands. They feel they are under great scrutiny from others. *Passivity experiences* – the sufferer's sensation of various bodily functions or movements being controlled by an external and irresistible force.	

Table 2.1.1

Positive and negative symptoms of schizophrenia

Who is affected by schizophrenia?
- Found worldwide, affecting 0.5–1% of the population.
- Equal incidence in men and women.
- Equal incidence across social classes.
- More sufferers found in urban areas.
- Onset peaks between 16–28 years and 30–45 years.

Causes

No one dominant causal factor for schizophrenia has emerged. However, some key pre-disposing, precipitating and perpetuating factors have been identified.

Genetic inheritance

The evidence that schizophrenia is partly hereditary is demonstrated by the fact that the risk of developing the illness increases from one in 100 to one in 10 if a close relative suffers from the condition. Twin studies show that monozygotic twins (from one egg) have a higher incidence rate than dizygotic twins (from two eggs). Adoptive studies – where offspring were separated at birth from one or both parents with schizophrenia – still show a higher incidence of developing the illness. However, as yet no specific gene has been identified.

Biochemical

The drugs used to control psychosis have led to the biochemical theory of its cause. Dopamine is a crucial neurotransmitter and anti-psychotic medication works by blocking dopamine receptors in the brain. The question arises as to whether an excess or imbalance of dopamine or a disruption of the chemical triggers in its production are responsible for the development of schizophrenia.

Brain damage

Recent scans have shown ventricular enlargement in the brains of some patients with schizophrenia. Other evidence includes abnormal EEGs and tests that show abnormal neurological signs. These findings are suggestive of early brain damage, before or soon after birth, but there is a lack of any consistent emergent pattern across sufferers of schizophrenia.

Stress

Evidence suggests that relapse, and occasionally onset of acute schizophrenia is triggered around the time of major life-events. Whether positive or negative in nature, these events hold the potential to be stressful. Family conflict, particularly the concept of 'high expressed emotion', where there is said to be excessive criticism and emotional dominance over the sufferer, has also been cited as precipitating breakdown. This can be an unhelpful and unsupportive concept if criticism of the family by professionals within psychiatry is implied: it can fail to acknowledge the strain placed on the family as they attempt to contain the disturbance of their relative. However, identification of 'high expressed emotion' can result in targeted family work, which has been shown to effectively reduce relapse rates.

Drug-induced schizophrenia
There is evidence to suggest that illicit drug use can precipitate a first schizophrenic breakdown and can be a trigger for subsequent relapses. The drugs in question include cannabis and LSD. It might be that some people are more susceptible to the chemical and psychological effects of these substances.

◄ Key points

> **What causes schizophrenia?**
> - There are a number of theories of cause, with no one dominant causal factor emerging:
>   – genetic inheritance
>   – biochemical factors
>   – brain damage
>   – stress
>   – illicit drug use.

Treatment

It is rare for sufferers of schizophrenia to present asking for help: in the acute stages the extreme effect of psychotic symptoms clouds their insight, and where onset is more insidious, social isolation has usually closed avenues for seeking treatment. There is no known cure and the treatment focuses on relieving or managing symptoms.

Anti-psychotic medication
This is given in response to acute symptoms, but also continued prophylactically in 'maintenance doses' to reduce the incidence of relapse. Anti-psychotic medications are also called neuroleptics and major tranquillizers (see Section 3.2, 'Anti-psychotic medication').

Admission to hospital
Sometimes this has to be compulsory under a section of the Mental Health Act in order to stabilize mood and contain behaviour. Before discharge occurs detailed systems for care in the community should be in place, with a clear indication of who is the key-worker co-ordinating care. All agencies involved in after-care should be informed of the discharge date and should be aware of the arrangements made.

Therapeutic environment
This helps to minimize the impact of acute psychotic symptoms. The presence of TV and radio can often influence and feed into delusions and hallucinations. Some sufferers find that the use of a stereo head-set playing soothing music helps to alleviate some of the torment of voices.

Supportive counselling

Counselling that is non-interpretative and non-probing in nature has been found to offer the most appropriate support. Sometimes this can include the whole family.

Daily occupation

This can provide structure and routine, which are important in keeping the negative symptoms of schizophrenia at bay and increasing self-esteem. Day hospital, day centre and sheltered work are examples of relevant activities. Equally important is structured social activity, which can be provided by a number of voluntary organizations and networks (see Section 3.3, 'Resources').

Accommodation and benefits

These are areas where professional help in organizing and claiming for entitlements is valuable. The disruption wrought by an acute schizophrenic breakdown sometimes results in the sufferer being made homeless and thus losing out on welfare rights. As well as social workers, there are several other advocacy agencies, specifically concerned with mental health issues.

Key points ➤

> **What can be done?**
> - Sufferers seldom seek help and treatment.
> - There is no known cure.
> - Treatment focuses on relief and management of symptoms:
>   - hospital admission
>   - therapeutic environment
>   - anti-psychotic medication
>   - community care co-ordinated by an identified staff member
>   - supportive counselling for sufferer and family
>   - structured daily occupation and social activity
>   - assistance with accommodation and benefits.

Schizophrenia and the role of the primary care nurse

The continuing policy to relocate care in the community has resulted in vastly increased numbers of people with schizophrenia being discharged from hospital. More than one-quarter no longer have contact with psychiatrists or community psychiatric nurses (CPN) and are cared for entirely by the general practitioner (GP) and primary services. The 'Care Programme Approach' introduced in the 1990s aims to ensure that all known patients with a severe and enduring illness are allocated a 'keyworker' who develops a detailed care plan with the patient and their family, or close support network. Negotiation and co-operation between services is a crucial element of this approach. It is an advantage that the primary health care team is situated in the community where the patient lives. They may be familiar with the patient's personal history, often from before schizophrenia developed, know other family members and have an understanding of the networks that can offer appropriate support.

Administration and management of anti-psychotic medication

An increasing number of practice nurses and district nurses have patients referred to them who require a regular injection of depot anti-psychotic medication. Also, many are involved in venepuncture to monitor blood serum levels of the oral anti-psychotic clozaril. Most patients state a preference for being treated at the GP's surgery; it is more easily accessible than a hospital, the appointment system is more flexible than a depot clinic or a CPN visit and certainly the stigma is less. For the primary care nurse, knowledge about the medication, its side-effects (see pp. 127–133) and appropriate administration technique is vital, but equally important is an awareness of the broader issues; the nature and course of schizophrenia and its management and the personal, social, medical and psychiatric history of the patient. Building up a relationship with the patient – even during the short time required for the administration of a depot or taking of blood – is of significant therapeutic value.

◄ *Key points*

> **The role of the primary care nurse**
> - 'Care in the community' has increased the numbers of patients with schizophrenia on GP lists.
> - Most patients state a preference for being treated at the GP's surgery.
> - Administration of depot anti-psychotic medication and venepuncture for serum levels of clozaril increasingly falls to primary care nurses.
> - Primary care nurses may be given identified roles within the 'care programme approach'.
> - Practice protocols should be developed to address the relevant issues of:
>   - poor attendance and non-compliance
>   - disturbed behaviour
>   - regular review of mental state and medication and side-effects
>   - liaison with secondary psychiatric services, other agencies and relatives
>   - health promotion and health screening.

Management issues

There are a number of issues around the management of patients with schizophrenia in a primary care setting that can usefully be addressed by practice protocols. Contributions and advice on the development of these could usefully be invited from workers from secondary psychiatric services.

Poor attendance and non-compliance

Poor insight and lethargy may result in erratic attendance, but equally it could be an early sign of relapse. The patient must always be followed up, if necessary, by a home visit, and the GP and any other key staff should be notified. Persistent non-compliance usually indicates the need for a referral to secondary psychiatric services.

Example of protocol if a patient does not attend (DNA)
- Same day – attempt to contact the patient (phone, note through door).
- Direct contact must be made within 4 days and *before* the weekend.
- Establish and document reason for DNA.
- Ensure that medication is given within 1 week of original appointment.
- Carry out or refer on for mental state assessment, if relevant.

Disturbed behaviour

Violent incidents with patients with schizophrenia are far more rare than the media would lead us to believe; however, it would be naive not to be prepared for this potential. It might be helpful to remember that an acutely disturbed patient is usually very frightened themselves. A calm response to them, despite the fear that their behaviour can generate, can be containing in itself. If the patient is an unknown quantity or has a history of disturbance it is advisable to have two members of staff present, or staff standing by, and to be in a room with access to an emergency buzzer. In these cases, home visits should not be undertaken alone. If the situation has escalated to this point the patient will need an urgent psychiatric assessment (see Chapter 3, 'Psychiatric assessment: management of aggression').

Regular review

The primary care nurse who sees patients regularly for their depot injection is in a good position to monitor for change in mental state and to record the positive and negative effects of medication regimes. While it would be wrong to suggest that the primary care nurse functions as a mental health specialist, the undertaking of basic reviews and referral to the GP for medication review fulfils a key function. It may be useful to note these reviews separately from the 'Lloyd George notes' in order to provide a clear picture and observe for changes over time. An example of a review sheet, which can be tucked into the main notes, appears in Section 3.1, 'Psychiatric assessment'.

Liaison

There are a number of services available to patients with schizophrenia, including secondary psychiatric services, specialist voluntary agencies and organizations and the patient's own circle of relatives and friends (the latter may well be much diminished due to the isolating nature of the condition). It is often unclear who has involvement in the patient's care and with regular contact the primary care nurse can usefully become the pivotal person who co-ordinates input. Inter-disciplinary team meetings can also provide a useful forum for co-ordinating care. Some patients will be discharged from hospital under the 'care programme approach'; primary care nurses may be asked to take on an identified role within this, in which case they must have copies of care plans and be involved in reviews and evaluations.

Health promotion and health screening
The mortality of sufferers of schizophrenia is double that of the normal population. There is a much higher incidence of cardio-vascular and respiratory disease, weight problems, smoking and alcohol addiction. Lack of insight and inertia may prevent them seeking help with physical difficulties. They are a prime target for both health promotion schemes and health screening programmes. In addition, secondary depression is often overlooked, despite the fact that it further pulls down the quality of life for the sufferer.

Fears about dealing with patients with schizophrenia
Fear of the unknown and fears fuelled by half-truth and exaggerated anecdotes are the experience of many a primary care nurse when it comes to dealing with patients with schizophrenia. This is understandable but need not and should not remain the situation (see Table 2.1.2).

Support groups, helplines and further information
Contact details and an explanation of the range of help and resources for each of the following organizations can be found in the 'A–Z of support groups', on pp. 134–154.

- African Caribbean Mental Health Association
- Hearing Voices Network
- The Mental Health Foundation
- MIND
- National Schizophrenia Fellowship
- Psychiatric Information Foundation UK (PIF-UK)
- Royal College of Psychiatrists
- SANELINE
- Vietnamese Mental Health Services
- Wales Mind Cymru
- The Zito Trust.

Common questions	Answers
• Isn't it best to avoid asking patients personal questions in case their reactions are more extreme or bizarre than I am able to cope with?	If the patient is acutely unwell it might be advisable to leave any stimulus, including asking questions, to a few experienced professionals involved in their care. However, as a general rule, sensitive, professional questioning will provide you with valuable information, while building a therapeutic relationship.
• Surely patients will be embarrassed if I ask them about the voices they hear?	Most people with schizophrenia are very familiar with their voices and won't feel embarrassed; some express relief that another person is aware and behaving in a matter of fact way about them.
• If I ask the patient directly about their voices or their delusional beliefs won't I be taking the lid off a can of worms?	These psychotic phenomena will be bubbling away under the surface anyway; talking about them may allow you some insight into thinking and underlying feelings and show them you are aware of the nature of their condition.
• What can I do if a patient becomes violent and smashes furniture or tries to hurt me?	This would be a rare occurrence. There would normally be some early warning signs, such as raised voice, threatening language, defensive posture. Do not continue with giving a depot, or whatever procedure you are embarking upon. Acknowledge their feelings of upset, explain that others might be able to help and call for assistance from colleagues. Protect yourself first and then from a position of safety try to get help to make the situation safe for others and the patient themselves.
• If I ask a patient whether they feel like harming themselves might I put the idea into their head and make them more likely to act on it?	No. If anything, the opportunity to admit to destructive feelings might well provide something of a safety valve. It is your responsibility to act on what they tell you and refer them urgently if expressing suicidal thoughts or giving other cause for concern. Ensure that all details are documented.
• If I ask specific questions about their psychiatric illness won't their expectations of me rise? Soon I'll be out of my depth and will let them down.	It is perfectly acceptable to admit that psychiatry is not your specialist field, but that as a nurse you can put them in contact with other professions who may be able to offer specific help.

Table 2.1.2

Common questions and answers about schizophrenia

CASE STUDY 2.1.1

Mrs Reynolds presents at the health centre asking to speak to someone about her son: she doesn't want to trouble the doctor because, 'it's not as though he's ill'. She is given an appointment with the practice nurse. She describes her son as intelligent – soon to sit A-levels – a quiet lad, who went regularly to chess club. Recently he's kept to his room and stopped eating with the family. She thought he was studying hard, but the college phoned to say that Andrew had not attended for 2 weeks and failed to hand in work. She went to confront him to find the room in disarray, curtains drawn in full daylight, and him lying on the bed staring and mumbling to himself.

What further questions might you ask Mrs Reynolds to broaden your picture of the situation?

- Did she speak to Andrew and how did he respond?
- How would she describe his character normally?
- Has anything happened recently that might be a trigger for his behaviour?
- Has she ever suspected him of experimenting with drugs?

Use her description of Andrew to try to identify pre-disposing factors and specific signs and symptoms of a mental illness.

- Teenager, facing the stressor of imminent exams, socially isolated, somewhat secretive in behaviour, self-neglect, possibly responding to auditory hallucinations.

What would be your plan of action?

- Refer to GP urgently for psychiatric assessment.

How would you explain this to Mrs Reynolds?

- Be as reassuring as possible – she suspects that her son needs help but resists the idea that he is ill.
- Acknowledge her obvious concern and anxiety.
- Affirm her feelings and support her judgement to seek help for her son.
- Establish that this is not your area of expertise and thus the need to refer on.
- Explain what is likely to happen for assessment to take place, including probable admission to psychiatric hospital.
- Offer to continue to see her and provide support for her.

CASE STUDY 2.1.2

A district nurse visits Miss Glade every week to dress her leg-ulcer wounds. She is a diabetic and has a history of schizophrenia, although she has remained well and out of hospital for over 10 years. The ulcer has deteriorated markedly, a change that Miss Glade refers to as 'ordained'. She explains that the weatherman forecast it on the TV and says 'we both know a time will come when I must act on his advice'.

What are the possible differential diagnoses?

- Toxic confusional state from wound infection;
- Diabetic confusional state, effect of hypoglycaemia;
- Relapse of schizophrenic illness;
- Other psychiatric condition – depression with psychotic features/signs of dementia.

How might you respond to the delusional ideas about her wound?

- Use gentle, non-confrontational ways of speaking.

- Ask in what way she intends to act on the weatherman's advice (i.e. ascertain whether she is in imminent danger of harming herself).
- Ask how all this makes her feel (i.e. ascertain mood: excited/angry/resigned, etc.).

Would you probe for more information, and if so, how might you question her?

- Ask whether she has touched the ulcer herself or done anything to it.
- Find out how she feels you can best help her.

What would be your plan of action?

- Swab wound, take body temperature.
- Check blood sugar status. NB: You may need to be sensitive and non-confrontational about gaining consent for and carrying out these procedures if the patient is showing signs of paranoia.
- Discuss urgently with GP and preferably arrange urgent joint visit.
- Identify any trigger for the situation – talk to the patient and friends/relatives if in contact.
- Check notes about the previous relapse to note any pattern of deterioration.
- Refer on to secondary psychiatric services, in most circumstances.

How would you explain this to Miss Glade?

- Express concern about her physical condition.
- Express concern about the anxiety/stress this might provoke in her.
- Float the idea that this might be an early sign of her becoming unstable again.
- Attempt to gain her acknowledgement that it would be good to 'nip this in the bud'.
- Promote the fact that you are her advocate, concerned with her best interests.

Reference

Roberts, G. (1996). Management of schizophrenia. *Practice Nursing*, 7, 13.

2.2 BI-POLAR AFFECTIVE DISORDER/ MANIC DEPRESSION

Definitions

Someone suffering from a bi-polar affective disorder may well have had a variety of titles given to their condition, manic depression being an equally common title. It is also sometimes referred to in the abbreviated form of affective disorder alone. Bi-polar affective disorder broadly describes a chronic and severe psychotic mental disorder where there are recurrent episodes of depression and mania affecting mood, thinking and behaviour. The terms 'bi-polar' and 'uni-polar' refer to the course of the disorder over time. Bi-polar is characterized by swings between episodes of depression and mania and uni-polar refers to suffering from recurrent bouts of depression alone. Recurrent episodes of mania alone are rare and tend to still be classified as bi-polar affective disorder. Hypomania is a term used to describe less severe manic episodes. Cyclothymic disorder describes less severe but still chronic fluctuations of mood between minor depression and hypomania over a number of years, where about 30% go on to develop full-blown bi-polar affective disorder.

◄ *Key points*

What is bi-polar affective disorder?
- 'Bi-polar' describes the two poles of the extremes of depression and mania.
- 'Affective' refers to mood.
- Bi-polar affective disorder is also known as manic depressive disorder.
- It is a psychotic mental disorder affecting mood, thinking and behaviour.
- Its course is chronic, characterized by recurrent swings between mania and depression.

Signs and symptoms

The main feature of a manic episode is elevated and excited mood. This differs from the commonly accepted expressions of intense joy or excitement that anyone might experience at some time, in that there is often an edge to it, where the sufferer may suddenly cry, become upset or easily and intensely irritable, to the point of displaying aggression with minimal provocation: this is known as 'labile mood'. The expansive mood can be very engaging to others: the sufferer's sense of well-being and high self-esteem – often at odds with their true circumstances – may veil the seriousness of their condition to the uninitiated and thus delay their urgent need for treatment. In this state they may express outlandish ideas or plan grand schemes and often spend large amounts of money using credit cards. Behaviour may be disinhibited, including sexually, and may lead to breaking the law. There is hyperactivity and easy distractibility accompanied by insomnia, where time is not taken to eat or care for themselves adequately (see Section 2.3 for the signs and symptoms of depression).

How sufferers are affected during a manic episode

- Mood: elevated and expansive
  irritable
  labile (move from happy to sad quickly, cry easily).
- Thought: flight of ideas (moving rapidly from topic to topic, where there is a link, but often only a tenuous one)
  grandiose delusions
  jealous or persecutory delusions.
- Speech: pressure of speech
  rapid speech
  loud voice/bursts of song
  clang association (stringing words together, that sound the same), punning and rhyming.
- Behaviour: disinhibited – sexually
  – aggressive
  overfamiliarity
  overactivity
  over-spending
  acting on wild plans or ideas
  distractibility.
- Bodily function: insomnia with little sign of exhaustion
  increased libido
  increased appetite
  weight loss.
- Perceptions: illusions where cues are misinterpreted
  lack of insight
  out of touch with reality
  hallucinations, auditory and visual (less common).

Differential diagnosis

Some organic conditions can produce symptoms of mania and must be ruled out at the initial stage: endocrine disorders such as Cushing's syndrome and thyroid problems are examples. Steroid-induced psychoses can also occur. Signs of mania may be present prior to a stroke and in some forms of epilepsy. Schizophrenia shares some of the psychotic features of bi-polar affective disorder, particularly persecutory hallucinations, and it is not uncommon for patients to have held both diagnoses within their psychiatric history.

Prognosis

It is possible to suffer an isolated incidence of hypomania – perhaps reactive to a stressful life event – but the lifetime prognosis following a first manic episode is poor, with 90–95% going on to experience further episodes of

mania and depression. With each episode experienced the probability of suffering a further episode increases, despite treatment. A common pattern has
been noted, in which the frequency and severity of episodes increase during the first five episodes, but then reach a plateau. However, it is possible
to remain well and stable for a long period of time – even years.

The risk of suicide is high: approximately 15% of sufferers actually kill
themselves and between 25% and 50% attempt suicide at least once. Deliberate and inadvertent self-harm during a manic phase is also a high risk.

The effect of manic episodes on the psychosocial world of the sufferer can be devastating. Interpersonal relationships can suffer hugely and
after a number of manic episodes irretrievable breakdown often occurs,
leaving the sufferer emotionally unsupported and uprooted from family
connections. Employment is disrupted, not only by absenteeism through
ill-health, but by inappropriate behaviour displayed at work during a manic
episode. Debt is often incurred during the manic phase and the consequences of disinhibited behaviour have to be faced, which may involve
legal proceedings. The consumption of large amounts of alcohol and taking illicit drugs is also common, both during a manic phase and increasingly as a way of life as they endure the process and effects of the disorder.

◀ Key points

The likely outcomes of bi-polar disorder
- Prognosis following a first manic episode is poor; 95% go on to experience the chronic cycle of mania and depression.
- Suicide risk is high: 25–50% attempt it, 15% actually kill themselves.
- Interpersonal relationships suffer severely; many break down irre-trievably.
- Employment is jeopardized.
- Financial problems are commonplace.
- Legal proceedings may ensue following inappropriate behaviour when manic.
- Alcohol abuse and illicit drug use is high.

Incidence and distribution

Bi-polar affective disorder affects about 1% of the population and is very
slightly more common in women. Onset usually occurs between the ages
of 20 and 30 years. Another surge has been noted amongst women between
35 and 45 years, where the pattern is of severe bouts of depression interspersed with less severe hypomanic episodes. Many studies show a higher
incidence in Britain amongst the upper social classes.

◀ Key points

Who is affected by bi-polar disorder?
- Affects 1% of the population.
- There is a slightly higher incidence in women.
- In Britain a higher incidence is shown in the upper classes.
- Onset commonly occurs between 20 and 30 years, with a further surge in women between 35 and 45 years.

Causes

Genetic

The clearest evidence of cause lies with genetic factors where bi-polar affective disorder can be clearly traced running through families. No single gene has been isolated as causal, but it is fair to say that family members can inherit a vulnerability to the condition.

Biological

Biological factors also appear to play a role, particularly relating to the endocrine system and hormonal control within the body. For women, the post-partum phase, soon after a baby is born, renders them particularly vulnerable to emotional lability and can precipitate a first manic episode known as puerperal psychosis.

Stress

Severe stress is often identified as a precipitating factor for both mania and depression, acting as the trigger to spark off an acute episode of either mood swing.

Negative life events

Traumatic events in childhood are sometimes identified as the antecedent to the later development of many mental disorders – bi-polar affective disorder included – but it is a difficult link to establish through scientific research and is thus a somewhat controversial theory.

Psychodynamic disturbance

Psychodynamic theory would also maintain that mania is an extreme reaction of denial to feelings and experience of sadness and depression.

Key points ➤

> **Suggested causes of bi-polar affective disorder**
> - Genetic factors
> - Biological factors
> - Stress vulnerability
> - Early psychological stress or trauma.

Treatment

Hospital admission

When a manic episode is in full flow it is almost always necessary to hospitalize the sufferer. Due to their lack of insight and their elevated sense of well-being, this may require compulsory admission under a section of the Mental Health Act.

Alternative residential admission

However, in some areas 'crisis houses' are available, where the individual 'checks in' when they recognize the early warning signs of an acute episode.

The focus is less on a medical model of treatment and more on provision of individualized social and emotional support, where self-management of the condition is emphasized. The Manic Depression Fellowship can provide details of 'crisis houses'.

Medication

Anti-psychotic and sedative medication is indicated in the acute phase and may be continued at maintenance doses (see Section 3.2, 'Anti-psychotic medication'). Longer-term medication treatment with mood-stabilizing drugs such as lithium salts, carbemazepine or sodium valporate may be started in order to prevent relapse. Lithium treatment requires regular blood screening for optimum therapeutic levels. Those on this treatment are closely monitored for signs of renal impairment and hypothyroidism.

Risk assessment

Deliberate and inadvertent self-harm risk assessment is crucial. In a manic state the sufferer is unpredictable and lacks the normal social constraints that usually curb excessive behaviour. If they are responding to delusions they may believe they have special powers that will protect them, when, in reality, they are exposing themselves to great danger.

Therapeutic environment

A therapeutic environment where external stimuli are limited allows the sufferer more chance to recover. Their distractibility means that the slightest interruption will rouse them from rest or disturb eating and drinking. High nutritional intake and rest and sleep are essential to allow the body to recover physically from a manic phase.

Emotional and practical support

The psychological support required by the sufferer and their loved ones cannot be overestimated. Following the manic phase, a period of time is often required to pick up the pieces: there may be impending legal proceedings to be faced, financial debts, difficulties related to employment and there may be a number of social indiscretions to be explained and mended. Many sufferers and their families express a need for an advocate and someone to liaise on their behalf. Specific voluntary groups and patient groups can prove invaluable at this time, both in a practical capacity and in offering more long-term psychological support.

Regrettably, in the past attention has focused almost exclusively on medication and hospitalization, but increasingly there is an awareness of the advantages of using a psycho-social framework for the care of sufferers from bi-polar affective disorder. Certainly, supportive counselling and cognitive behavioural therapy (see 'Glossary') have been shown to contribute greatly in improving the long-term prognosis for this condition. Self-management can also greatly reduce the risk of relapse when the individual learns to avoid particular stressors and to recognize their own early warning signs and present for treatment and support in good time.

Treatment and management
- Anti-psychotic and sedative medication – immediate
  - maintenance
- Hospitalization – by compulsory section if necessary
- Deliberate self-harm risk assessment
- Therapeutic environment with removal of stimuli
- Help with self-care, where mania can dangerously exhaust body and mind
- Psychological support for sufferer and family
- Monitor for depression after manic episode
- Professional intervention, where legal proceedings and debts have occurred as a result of mania
- Referral to voluntary organisations for information and support
- Some studies show that use of cognitive behaviour therapy helps to reduce relapse rate and increase medication compliance.

The role of the primary health care nurse

It will probably be relatively rare in a primary care setting to be confronted by a person in the acute stages of a manic episode. However, awareness of the stress caused by life-events, and that the individual's experience of this can be severe enough to precipitate a mental disorder, is perhaps more important for primary health care workers to be aware of than for any other group: you are on the 'front line' and an appropriate, professional response is the first requirement in treatment.

In the less acute phase primary care nurses may well be carrying out venepuncture for lithium salt levels. Awareness of the medication and side-effects and the long-term nature of prophylactic maintenance medication is important if support is to be offered with compliance (see Section 3.2, 'Anti-psychotic medication'). Also, regular patient visits for venepuncture offer the opportunity for a review of mental state and are an invaluable asset when passed on to secondary psychiatric services to provide an accurate overview of the patient's care and the best course it should follow (see Section 3.1, 'Psychiatric assessment').

A familiarity with the work of specific national voluntary organizations and their local off-shoots is most useful. The Manic Depression Fellowship (MDF) is the main organization in this country and their major remit is to offer support and to foster the skills required for self-management. You can work with the patient to recognize signs that they are becoming 'high' or 'low' – especially as insight is often an early casualty to mania.

The key to managing your condition successfully is to understand how it uniquely affects you.

MDF leaflet

The high levels of illicit drug and alcohol abuse in this patient group make them an obvious target for health promotion campaigns, indeed episodes of heavy substance use may serve to flag up the likelihood of impending mania or depression. You can provide support in weaning dependence from drugs and alcohol and offer more positive coping strategies as an alternative to this abuse.

◄ Key points

What can you do?
- Be aware that the stress caused by life events can extend into a mental disorder.
- Administer venepuncture for lithium levels.
- Give support with maintenance of medication compliance.
- Liaise with secondary psychiatric services.
- Refer to appropriate voluntary organizations.
- Give advice about health promotion.
- Help the patient to recognize signs of impending mania or depression.
- Encourage self-management.

Support groups, helplines and further information

Contact details and an explanation of the range of help and resources for each of the following organizations can be found in the 'A–Z of support groups', on pp. 134–154.

- African Caribbean Mental Health Association
- Chinese Mental Health Association
- Manic Depression Fellowship
- The Mental Health Foundation
- MIND
- Psychiatric Information Foundation UK (PIF-UK)
- Royal College of Psychiatrists.

CASE STUDY 2.2.1

An occupational health nurse at an advertising agency is taken aside in the staff cafeteria by a senior member of staff concerned about a member of her team. The young man in question is sitting with colleagues, not eating but speaking animatedly and causing a great deal of appreciative laughter. He is attracting attention from around the room because of the loudness of his voice and the fact that he keeps jumping to his feet and is clearly 'playing to the gallery'. She explains to the nurse that he has great promise; is full of ideas and energy and she admits she pushes him hard because he produces such good work. However, in the last few days his behaviour has given cause for concern. Last night he stayed at work, had clearly not slept and the cleaners complained of full coffee cups left at all the desks this morning. He adamantly refused to go home and was rather rude. He said he didn't need sleep and when he shared his current work ideas with her they seemed less inspirational and more outlandish and bizarre. A group meeting is scheduled for the afternoon with a valued client and she is anxious that he is prevented from attending.

How might you tackle this situation?

- Safeguard the short-term welfare of the employee by:
  - getting him away from the immediate stimuli perpetuating and exacerbating his condition
  - establishing the severity of his condition and referring on for appropriate treatment
  - preventing his attendance at the meeting and hopefully avoiding playing into any paranoid delusions that this may spark.
- In terms of staff education about stress at work:
  - at management level emphasize the responsibility for junior staff and for personal welfare of *all* staff members
  - health promotion, e.g. setting up relaxation classes, etc.
  - lobby senior management for staff facilities and perks to minimize or counteract stress.

Itemize the signs and symptoms of a manic phase evident in this scenario.

- Elevated and expansive mood, loud speech, excitability, distractibility – not eating or drinking, hyperactivity, insomnia, wild plans and ideas, aggressive edge.

What questions might you ask to elicit further evidence?

- Up-front questions about any psychiatric history of previous manic or depressive episodes, current medication.
- Establish whether he is suffering delusions (i.e. question him about how important he believes he is, does he have any ideas about being on a mission, etc.).
- Question regarding any recent stressful life events or anniversaries of life events/work pressures.
- Check physical health status.
- Check whether he is taking drugs or alcohol.

Who might you refer on to?

- The GP.
- Family/friends/next of kin (taking into account confidentiality issues).

CASE STUDY 2.2.2

On Monday morning a health visitor finds a number of messages on the office answer phone from a newly referred client – Mrs Hillary Fenton – whom she had visited for the first time the previous Friday. Mrs Fenton is 2 weeks post-delivery of her first child, a healthy baby boy. The health visitor had found Mrs Fenton slightly edgy, which she had put down to the fact that her husband was returning to work from paternity leave on the Monday morning.

The following are excerpts from the messages, which took up the entire tape:

You should know for your records we've re-named our first-born. He is Isaac.

I'm just phoning to ask if you could come as soon as possible. I need to check everything I'm doing is perfect for Isaac.

I forgot to mention about Isaac, that it is his destiny – destinstar – which we denied, but there's no dodging it . . . hedge it, fudge it, gadgets, and nets, twitchy nets. Greg [husband] says 'sod it'; he doesn't realize the honour bestowed upon our first born – called Samuel, now, and always, happy ever after to be Isaac.

There might be sacrifices to be made – honey and spices – sugar and spice and all things nice.

What would you suggest as the health visitor's immediate plan of action?

Place in a hierarchy of urgency and give reasons for each suggestion.
- Establish date and time of messages – you need to know at what point in the weekend this crisis was unfolding.
- Immediately and urgently inform the GP – there is enough information on the tape to confirm that Mrs Fenton has severe psychotic symptoms, that she may be in danger of harming the baby (references to sacrifice), that her husband may be dismissive or unaware of the severity of her disturbance and that she herself is attempting to get help by making so many calls to the health visitor. Save the tape as evidence of her symptoms.

Can you name some of the psychotic phenomenon evident in this tape?

- 'Desinstar' = neologism
- 'Dodge it, hedge it, fudge it, gadgets' = clang association
- 'Gadget and nets, twitchy nets' = word association, flight of ideas
- 'Sacrifices to be made – honey and spices – sugar and spice and all things nice' = clang association, word association, flight of ideas
- Grandiose delusions about the cosmic importance of her son.

Is it possible to make any sense of Mrs Fenton's disordered thoughts?

This might be useful if she is referred back to you in the future. They may represent genuine areas of concern, which became distorted by her puerperal psychosis, but about which she can seek reassurance and advice when she is well.
- There are religious references and obsession with sacrifice.
- She may fear that her child will be taken from her or harmed in some way.
- She may be concerned about the sacrifices she will have to make for her baby.
- Some things she said suggest areas of disharmony with her husband.
- She expresses anxieties about doing her best for the baby.
- The 'sugar and spice' reference is from a nursery rhyme about baby girls. Hers is a boy, who, according to the same rhyme, are made of 'slugs and snails.' Is there an issue here about the preferred gender of her child?
- 'Twitchy nets' may allude to nosy neighbours and concerns about the attitude of others towards her. This might be uppermost in her concerns after a psychiatric hospital admission.

2.3 DEPRESSION

Definition of depression

Depression is a very common mental disorder in the general population. It is also commonly confused with other normal mood reactions where lowering of mood is a feature. Depression and sadness are not the same thing, even though the phrase 'feeling depressed' is widely used to describe feeling sad or unhappy. Everybody feels sad and unhappy from time to time. These reactions are normal and often understandable given the circumstances with which they are associated. Ordinary, reactive feelings of sadness and unhappiness usually end when the cause of the reaction disappears or is dealt with. This is different to depression where the sadness is persistent. Depression is characterized by a pervasive, on-going low mood, a lack of or reduced sense of enjoyment of life and a pattern of negative thinking.

Another significant characteristic of depression is that it sometimes presents in the form of physical symptoms, such as 'pain', fatigue or headaches rather than as emotional symptoms. Depression can be a main presenting problem in primary care settings but it can also be a secondary problem that results from the experience of another physical or psychiatric disorder. It is also important to bear in mind that while emotional symptoms, such as low mood, are commonly reported by people presenting in primary health care settings, they do not necessarily mean that the patient has a psychiatric problem.

Key points ➤

What is depression?
- It is more than being 'sad' or 'feeling down'.
- It is a mood, or affective, disorder characterized by pervasive low mood, negative thinking and lack of enjoyment of life.
- Presentation in primary health care settings is often through physical symptoms.
- Most people recover fully, though depression tends to be recurrent.
- Treatment shortens the duration of a depressive episode.

Prognosis

People who become depressed can be expected to make a full recovery. However, prognosis differs depending on the type and severity of the individual's depression. Most single episodes of depression last between 3 and 8 months. Only a small percentage of people remain depressed for longer than this. While depression is a time-limited problem it is also a recurrent one. Recurrent episodes of depression are more likely to be experienced by people who have more severe symptoms. It is also the case that people report that they experience progressively more severe symptoms in recurrent episodes and that their depression-free periods become progressively shorter. Appropriate treatment can significantly shorten the natural course of an individual's depression.

People who experience depression have a higher suicide risk than the general population, though the risk is again much higher in people who experience their symptoms as 'severe' (see Section 2.6, 'DSH/suicide', pp. 73–81).

Signs and symptoms

There are a number of ways of describing depression and it may, in fact, be better to talk about depressive illnesses as a way of acknowledging the different presentations and symptom spectrum. While the classification systems and diagnostic criteria refer to 'mild' and 'severe' depression in terms of the existence or absence of specific biological and psychological symptoms, it is worth noting that people experience their symptoms in individual and subjective ways. A person with an objectively 'mild' depression may cope less well and find their life disrupted more by it than an individual with the symptoms of an apparently 'severe', ongoing depression.

Table 2.3.1, the classification table overleaf, outlines the signs and symptoms associated with different types of diagnosis, though the extent to which they represent distinctly different forms of depressive illness remains debatable. The core symptoms of any form of depression include:

- Biological features: changes (positive or negative) in sleep, appetite, weight, energy, and physical activity
- Cognitive features: reduced attention, concentration, and decision-making abilities, increased negative thoughts
- Emotional features: reduced feelings of enjoyment and satisfaction and a persistently low mood
  increased anxiety, irritability, agitation.

The above descriptions are of the symptoms of uni-polar depressive disorders. For a diagnosis of primary depression they should not primarily be due to the use or abuse of drugs and should also cause distress or impairment in social or occupational functioning.

Depression is also a feature of bi-polar disorder (for a more detailed discussion see Section 2.2, 'Bi-polar affective disorder/manic depression', pp. 25–33).

Depression in minority ethnic groups

Members of minority ethnic groups can present with the typical symptoms of major depressive illness. They are, however, also likely to present with somatic symptoms and are more likely to express feelings of shame rather than guilt.

In a study of an inner city setting, Shaw *et al.* (1999) found that symptoms of depressive disorders were more prevalent in African Caribbean women than in white European women and that while medical help seeking was similar in both groups, African Caribbeans with symptoms of mental disorder were more likely to seek additional help from other sources.

Table 2.3.1

Classification of depression
(adapted from ICD-10)

Classification	Also known as . . .	Signs and symptoms
Major depressive disorder	Endogenous/severe	Over at least a 2-week period: • Low mood most of the day, nearly every day. Often lowest in the morning. • Shows markedly less interest, pleasure in or motivation towards nearly all activities most of the day, nearly every day. Plus at least four of the following: • Reduced or absent libido. • Experiences 5% or more change in weight (up or down), or significant change in appetite (up or down) nearly every day. • Experiences significant change in sleep pattern (insomnia or, less often, hypersomnia) nearly every day, typically early morning waking. • Physically agitated or retarded nearly every day. • Experiences fatigue/loss of energy nearly every day. • Experiences reduced concentration, thinking and decision-making ability nearly every day. • Preoccupation with worthlessness, guilt and/or hopelessness about self, future or the world generally. • Recurrent thoughts about death, and/or suicide with or without making a plan.
Mild depression	Reactive/neurotic	• Low mood most of the day, nearly every day. Often lowest in the morning. Not as persistent as above. • Agitation, irritability or other anxiety symptoms At least two of the following also experienced over a 2-week period: • Change in normal sleep pattern (initial anxiety-based insomnia and subsequent oversleeping). • Loss of enjoyment and motivation. • Pattern of negative thinking about self, future or the world generally. • Reduced attention and concentration. • Feelings of guilt and worthlessness. • Headaches, general but vague body pains.

Depression in older (elderly) people

As above, older people may present with typical symptoms of major and mild depression. They may also present with agitation, confusion and memory disturbance that can appear like early onset dementia rather than depression. While organic changes should be investigated, depression should not be overlooked as a possible, and more optimistic, explanation of mood and behaviour change.

Post-natal depressive disorders

Post-natal 'blues' and post-natal depression are forms of depressive disorder that occur in the post-partum period. Post-natal, or 'maternity' blues is a relatively common experience and involves a mild elevation in mood immediately following childbirth. Post-natal blues tend to last between

3 and 5 days. The symptoms presented are irritability, lowering of mood and feelings of inadequacy. Women with a history of pre-menstrual mood problems seem to be more at risk of developing post-natal 'blues'. However, the 'blues' are self-limiting with no specific intervention, other than social and emotional support and listening, being required.

Post-natal depression is a more severe, and relatively less common, form of post-partum depressive disorder. The signs and symptoms of major depressive disorder or mild depression tend to occur in the 6 weeks after the birth. Post-natal depression can persist and affect everyday functioning and mother–child relationships if untreated. Social and emotional factors (see below), in particular close supportive relationships, family history and marital conflict, are important predisposing and precipitating factors.

Bereavement reactions
Grief reactions and the low, and sometimes hopeless, mood associated with the loss of a loved one are natural feelings. While a person's mood may be low for a period of time, they should not be treated for a clinical depression.

Differential diagnosis
It is not always easy to distinguish the symptoms of depression from normal fluctuations in mood or natural grief responses where a loss or bereavement has been experienced. Knowledge of the individual combined with careful assessment and history taking should help to rule out other conditions and problems that can mimic depression. The key assessment strategy is to look for a pattern of biological and psychological signs and symptoms existing with low mood together (see 'Signs and symptoms' above), rather than to use 'low mood' as a single, defining factor. Care must be taken to rule out:

- the effects of using or misusing illicit drugs, alcohol or prescribed medication
- reactions to chronic physical illness
- the flattened affect and motor retardation associated with schizophrenia
- physical illnesses such as Addison's disease, Cushing's disease, electrolyte disturbance or vitamin and mineral deficiencies.

Incidence and distribution
Depressive illnesses are amongst the most common mental health problems affecting people in the UK, and indeed throughout the world. The risk of experiencing depression is higher for women than it is for men. Lifetime risk is approximately 5–12% for men but double that for women.

	Factor	More likely	Less likely
Table 2.3.2	Sex	Women	Men
Risk factors influencing susceptibility to depression	Class	Working	Middle
	Location	Urban	Rural
	Age	Late twenties onwards	Adolescence to early adulthood
	Women	With young children	No young children
		Married	Unmarried
	Men	Unmarried	Married
	Home status	Live alone	Live with others/partner
	'Loss' events	Recent	Non-recent
	History	Previous episodes	No previous history
	Physical health	Chronic, disabling, painful condition or unexplained symptoms	Good physical health

Causes

Depression is not a character flaw or the fault of the individual concerned. It is important to identify, acknowledge and try to understand a person's depression rather than fob them off with the dismissive view that it's just a minor, passing or self-indulgent emotional state caused by either of these factors. Depression is also not a purely biochemical or medical disorder. There are a number of known biological, psychological and social factors involved in causing depression, though each individual will experience a unique combination of trigger factors. Depression is complex and perplexing because it is very difficult to identify a single causal factor in any individual's experience of it.

Biological factors

Twin and adoption studies reveal that people do inherit some predisposition to depression. The genetic link is much stronger for bi-polar disorder than for uni-polar depression.

Medical studies have also demonstrated that biochemical factors do play some role in depression. Monoamine metabolites, especially noradrenaline and serotonin in the cerebrospinal fluid and urine, are reduced in people with depression. Anti-depressant medications are designed to increase the monoamine availability. People who experience a reduction in these neurotransmitter substances experience physiological effects such as disturbed sleep, changes in appetite and levels of energy and concentration. The precise action and effects of these biochemical factors remains unclear.

Physical illnesses

The symptoms of depressive illness are a common feature of a number of physical diseases. In such situations depressive disorder is a secondary problem resulting from the primary physical illness. Wilkinson (1989) identifies the following as being particularly significant in this respect:

- Neurological diseases: dementia
epilepsy
multiple sclerosis
Parkinson's disease
stroke.
- Malignant diseases: brain tumours
cancer of the pancreas
lung cancer.
- Endocrine diseases: Addison's disease
Cushing's disease
hypothyroidism.
- Kidney disease: kidney dialysis
kidney failure.
- Anaemia: folate deficiency
iron deficiency;
vitamin B_{12} deficiency.
- Infectious diseases: brucellosis
glandular fever
hepatitis
shingles
influenza.

Stress reactions/life events
Mild, or so-called 'reactive', depression is frequently caused by a notable event in the individual's life. There are a wide variety of possible life transitions (leaving home, getting married, giving birth, retirement) and unexpected life events (bereavement, major illness, divorce) that can cause the individual to experience a level of stress that pushes them into depression. A combination of stressful life events (such as bereavement, unemployment, relationship breakdown) over a short period of time is more likely to expose an individual's vulnerability to depression than a single event. It is important to establish the meaning of a life event for the individual concerned. What may appear as an apparently trivial event to an 'objective' observer may have enormous significance to the person who experiences it, especially where a 'loss' also threatens the person's sense of identity or psychological security in some way.

Relationship factors
Individuals who have confiding, supportive relationships with an intimate partner seem less likely to experience depression than individuals who lack such support. Unbalanced relationships, where one partner is more dominant than the other, require one of the individuals to adjust and accept a submissive, lesser role and may have a negative impact on their self-esteem and sense of self-worth. This increases vulnerability to depression. In a classic study of the social origins of depression, Brown and Harris (1978) identified social factors, such as major life events, as precipitating depression, and a number of other social factors as predisposing, or

vulnerability, factors in depression. The Brown and Harris (1978) study identified working class women, particularly those who were lone parents, as being particularly 'at risk'. The four key vulnerability factors that appeared to predispose this group to depressive disorder were:

- loss of their own mother before the age of 11
- having 3 or more children under the age of 14 at home
- the lack of a supportive, confiding relationship
- the lack of employment outside of the home.

Drugs

Many prescribed medications (for example, corticosteroids and some oral contraceptives) have direct depression-inducing side-effects. The negative, uncomfortable side-effects of other medications might also indirectly lead to an individual feeling unhappy, irritable and ultimately depressed. Misuse of, and withdrawal from, non-prescribed drugs, such as street amphetamines, barbiturates and ecstasy, can predispose an individual to depression. Alcohol is a known mood suppressant.

Learned behaviour

'Learned helplessness' is a phenomenon identified by Seligman (1975), which he related to depression. It is suggested that helplessness may become a learned response to situations where a person feels helpless when subject to 'threats' or stress outside of their control or perceived influence. A family history of depressive illness may partly be accounted for by genetic inheritance but might also partly be explained on the grounds of the individual having learned inappropriate, maladaptive or poor coping responses when faced by difficult or threatening situations. It is also possible that people acquire, or learn, habitually negative patterns of thinking that predispose them to depressive illness.

Organizing the causes

The brief outline of the various causes of depressive disorders given above is often organized into a 'stress–vulnerability' model. This is based on the

Key points ➤

> **What causes depression?**
> - The 'stress–vulnerability' model is the most commonly held explanation.
> - Predisposing factors include genetic inheritance, family relationships and learned behaviour.
> - Precipitating factors include high stress/life events, physical illness, substance misuse and lack of emotional and social support.
> - There is no dominant causal factor and each individual's depression has its own unique causal pattern.

assertion that predisposing (vulnerability) factors make an individual more likely to experience depressive disorder, but that this will only be precipitated by the presence of 'stress' factors. All sorts of events or circumstances can act as stress factors. The individual's ability to cope with the stress and the way that they perceive the factors and their ability to deal with them are crucial to progress.

Treatment of depressive illness

There are a wide variety of methods of both preventing and combating depressive illness. Depressive illness can generally be managed in primary health care settings, though a large proportion of depression remains undiagnosed and is self-managed. Research evidence suggests that the most effective treatment involves a combination of medication and behaviour therapy.

Medication

Anti-depressant medication treats the symptoms, not the causes of depressive illness. They may be used to 'kick start' or speed up the natural recovery process and can provide enough of a boost to enable individuals to help themselves. Anti-depressants have a 60–70% response rate in people with major depression but are said to fail frequently because of under-dosage or compliance problems. Anti-depressants, like many other drugs, can have unpleasant side-effects that make them unacceptable to some patients and causes compliance problems. GPs and psychiatrists will sometimes continue prescribing anti-depressants for up to 6 months after an individual's first episode of depression has resolved. This has been shown to reduce the relapse rate and can also have a preventive effect in individuals who have recurrent depressive episodes.

Anti-depressants may be contra-indicated in women with post-natal depression who wish to continue breast feeding as they are excreted in breast milk.

Social and emotional support

People who have a supportive social network can often use their relationships with others to disclose and talk through the thoughts and feelings that are part of their depressive illness. The sense of belonging and emotional security that can be derived from being part of a supportive group, such as a family or club, can contribute positively to a person's self-esteem and sense of self-worth. However, an individual may also feel that they are unable to share their feelings and problems with people who are close to them or may have found that this hasn't helped in any significant way.

Talking therapies

Every primary health care practitioner can help to improve the mood of an individual with a depressive disorder simply by providing them with the opportunity and time to talk and by listening. Cognitive behaviour therapy

(CBT), often in combination with medication, has been shown to be effective in the treatment of depression but is likely to require referral to a specialist practitioner of CBT. This person is likely to be a psychiatric nurse or clinical psychologist working in the local mental health services. General counselling is not an effective treatment for depressive disorder itself but may be useful and helpful for people with more pronounced anxiety symptoms.

Women experiencing post-natal depression may benefit from a form of talking therapy, depending on the precipitating and maintaining factors in their depression. Marital therapy, cognitive behaviour therapy or supportive counselling may be appropriate.

Table 2.3.3

Approaches to types of talking therapy

Type of talking therapy	Basic approach
Cognitive behaviour therapy	Identification and modification of negative patterns of thinking.
Psychodynamic/psychoanalytic therapy	Analysis of an individual's early experiences, parental influences and relationship dynamics.
Counselling/person-centred therapy	Problem identification, development of self-knowledge and supported guidance to identify personal solutions and resources to address problems.

Complementary therapies

Therapies such as acupuncture, massage, homeopathy, reflexology and herbalism have been found to be useful in reducing some of the symptoms of depression and can also be used in a preventative way. These therapies are typically provided on a fee-paying basis by private sector practitioners, though their availability in NHS primary health care settings is increasing. Relaxation methods, such as progressive muscle relaxation or guided-fantasy, can be self-taught or learnt by attending an adult education class. Books and tapes providing suitable information and materials are often available from local authority libraries or can be purchased from high street shops.

ECT

Electro-convulsive therapy (ECT) is a controversial treatment for depressive illnesses. It tends to be used in specialist psychiatric services and is uncommon in primary health care settings. ECT is used in cases of severe depression where there are clear, significant biological symptoms such as psychomotor retardation.

Key points ➤

What can be done?
- Patients are sometimes reluctant to acknowledge the mood component of their depression.
- CBT and anti-depressant medication are the most effective treatments.
- Depression does resolve in time.
- Addressing the factors that have caused or that are maintaining the depression is more important than concentrating on the mood itself.
- Emotional and social support are very important in providing the conditions for recovery.

Depression and the role of the primary care nurse

Risk management

Risk assessment of people who present with a clear depressive illness should focus on the possibility of self-neglect, self-harming behaviour (including excessive alcohol use and drug misuse) and suicide. Risk assessment and management should begin as soon as a depressive illness is suspected.

Recognizing depression

Primary health care nurses play an important role in identifying depressive illness in service users. It is good practice to actively screen people who belong to one of the high risk groups for depression. These include older (elderly) people, single mothers with young children, people who have experienced a number of adverse, recent life events and people who have significant physical health problems. Freeman (1993) warn against imposing 'understandability' criteria, which can be a barrier to recognizing the symptoms of depression in these and other groups. The reasons for an individual's depression don't have to be logical and immediately understandable as a 'good cause' for a problem to exist. The pattern of core symptoms alone should be sufficient to alert you to the possibility of a depressive illness.

People are more likely to present with physical or somatic symptoms than with specifically mood-related complaints. Pain and fatigue ('tired all the time') are the most common somatic presentations. Neither of these symptoms are, however, sufficient in themselves (even in the absence of physical illness) to indicate depression. Freeman *et al.* (1993) suggest that patients who present somatically are not reluctant to admit to depressive symptoms if asked directly about them. Armstrong (1995) has developed a question-based flow chart to aid the recognition of depression by nurses in primary health care settings (see p. 44).

Treatment strategy	Indications	Nurse's role
Medication	Moderate and severe depressive disorders.	Information-giving about usage, effects and side-effects.
Talking therapies	Supportive counselling for 'mild' depressive disorders, CBT for more severe and enduring depressive disorders.	Listening and supportive interventions in mild depressive disorder. Referral or information regarding other talking therapy options, unless specifically trained and supervised to deliver them.
Social and emotional support	Any form of depressive disorder.	Information about local and other resources, development of supportive relationship with patient.
Complementary therapies	Presentations of depressive disorders where anxiety is a significant or co-existing feature.	Referral or information regarding therapy options, unless specifically trained and supervised to deliver them.
Self-help	Any form of depressive disorder.	Information regarding resources and strategies and basic emotional support to reinforce personal efforts and self-help motivation.

Table 2.3.4

Dealing with depressive illness

Figure 2.3.1

Recognizing depression (Source: Armstrong, 1995)

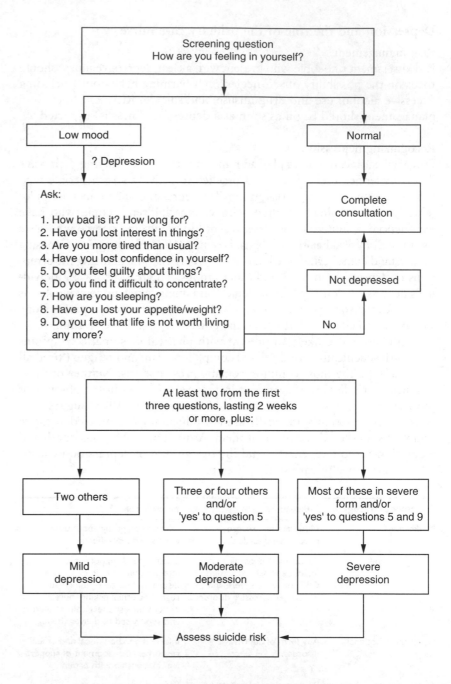

Treatment and referral

People who are diagnosed as having a depressive illness in primary care settings are generally treated with one or more of the treatment strategies outlined in Table 2.3.4, each of which has implications for the role of primary health care nurses.

Support groups, helplines and further information

Contact details and an explanation of the range of help and resources for each of the following organizations can be found in the 'A–Z of support groups' on pp. 134–154.

General
- Chinese Mental Health Association
- Depression Alliance
- The Mental Health Foundation
- MIND
- Psychiatric Information Foundation UK (PIF-UK)
- Relate (National Marriage Guidance)
- Royal College of Psychiatrists
- SANELINE
- Seasonal Affective Disorders Association (SAD).

Bereavement
- The Compassionate Friends
- Cruse Bereavement Care
- Foundation for the Study of Infant Deaths
- National Association of Bereavement Services
- Still-birth and Neonatal Death Society (SANDS)
- Sudden Death Support Association.

Post-natal
- Association for Post-natal Illness
- See SANDS above.

CASE STUDY 2.3.1

Derek Farmer is a 32-year-old social worker, currently on sick leave from his job as a care manager working with children. Derek has come in for a meeting with his line manager and the occupational health nurse as he has gradually extended his sick leave without providing a sick note from his GP. Derek arrives 15 minutes late, looking unkempt, tired and quite anxious. He says several times that he is sorry for not letting people know about his plans, that he is not coping very well at the moment because 'everything is going wrong for me', and that he just needs a bit more time to sort things out. Derek says that he wonders why he can't sleep even though he feels tired all the time.

What else would you ask of Derek in order to gain a more complete understanding of his current feelings and circumstances?

- An explanation of the 'things' he refers to.
- How Derek explains his recent 'not coping' and need for sick leave.
- about recent life events or sources of stress.
- to describe his current feelings and plans with regard to work.

Which features of Derek's presentation would alert you to the possibility that he may be experiencing a depressive disorder?

- His negative thinking, his unkempt appearance (if uncharacteristic), his agitated behaviour and apparent poor coping.

How might you respond to Derek's question about why he can't sleep even though he feels tired all the time?

- Explore this further, asking Derek to describe the nature of his sleep problems and about current activity pattern and energy levels.
- Suggest that they may be the symptoms of illness and that GP assessment would clarify this.

What else, apart from sleeping tablets, would you suggest to Derek as being a way of overcoming his current problems?

- A GP appointment for mental health assessment.
- Cognitive behaviour therapy referral/assessment.
- Information/advice on depressive disorders.

CASE STUDY 2.3.2

Monica Roberts is a 28-year-old lone parent of three children. Her youngest child is 9 months old, her other two are 2 and 3 years old. Monica is a regular visitor to the surgery. While talking to the health visitor, who inquired about her baby's recent sleep problems, Monica complained that even when the baby does sleep through the night, she is awake herself and can't go to sleep because she is worried about him. She says that she never worried so much about her other two but that she has become preoccupied that her latest baby may become unwell and that she won't notice. At the same time, Monica confides, she feels angry with the baby.

Monica doesn't know what to do about this. She says that it is affecting her health, as she feels very tired, unhappy and thinks about very little else. She wonders whether it would be worth having the baby 'checked out' again.

What are the possible reasons for the apparent change in Monica's mental state at this time?
- Post-natal depression
- Pressures of three children and possible lack of emotional support/practical help
- Undetected physical illness
- Recent stressful life events.

Which features of Monica's presentation fit the core symptoms of depression?

- Persistent sadness, sleep disturbance, preoccupation/negative pattern of thinking, poor decision-making abilities.

What other information about the situation would you wish to obtain from Monica?

- Current sources of support/daily contact with other people, history of current worries, length of time she's felt low/last time she gained enjoyment from something, current coping strategies.

Monica asks you why she feels so angry and guilty about her feelings towards her youngest child. How would you respond?

- Explore the nature of the anger/thoughts/behaviour that go with it.
- Suggest that her frustration is/should be with the situation, not with the baby.
- Discuss possible coping strategies that address lack of support/negative thinking.
- Raise the possibility of a depressive episode as an explanation and as something that can be resolved.

What would you suggest to Monica that might help her to deal with these problems?

- Undergo an assessment for depressive disorder.
- Use/develop her social and family network where possible to gain social contact and emotional support.
- Consider a short course of anti-depressants if indicated by her assessment.
- Offer supportive counselling opportunities if Monica wishes and lacks a supportive social network.
- Give information about local community resources and any appropriate national services that can offer support.

Resources

Information can be obtained from the National Depression Care Training Centre, Nene University College, Boughton Green Road, Northampton NN2 7AL. Tel: 01604 735 500.

The purpose of this centre is to provide a training course for all primary care nurses in recognizing and managing depression in primary care. The course is accredited with 5 CATS points and is designed for RGNs working in community and primary care settings.

References

Armstrong, E. (1995). *Mental Health Issues in Primary Care*. Basingstoke: Macmillan.

Brown, G.W. and Harris, T.O. (1978). *Social Origins of Depression*. London: Tavistock.

Freeman, C. (1993). *Depressive Illness: A Critical Review of Current Practice and the Way Ahead*. Edinburgh: The Scottish Office Clinical Resource and Audit Group.

Seligman, M.E.P. (1975). *Helplessness: On Depression, Development and Death*. San Francisco: W.H. Freeman.

Shaw, C.M., Creed, F., Tomenson, L., Riste, L., Cruikshank, J.K. and Rait, G. (1999). Prevalence of anxiety and depressive illness and help seeking behaviour in African Caribbeans and white Europeans: two-phase general population survey. *British Medical Journal*, 318, 302–306.

Wilkinson, D.G. (1989). *Depression: Recognition and Treatment in General Practice*. Oxford: Radcliffe Medical Press.

2.4   ANXIETY DISORDERS

Definition

Anxiety is a normal, commonly experienced response to stress, which generally enhances an individual's physical and intellectual performance. The Yerkes–Dobson curve indicates that low anxiety leads to low performance levels, increasing anxiety stimulates increasing performance and that too much anxiety will result in a deterioration in performance. Everyone has his or her own curve with a point at which anxiety becomes a problematic and negative influence on performance. Problematic levels of anxiety have a detrimental effect on a person's ability to function physically, socially and intellectually and induce an unpleasant emotional state. Anxiety disorders are relatively common and are typically under-diagnosed in primary care settings.

Anxiety problems are characterized by a prevailing feeling of apprehension that can be felt, on a continuum, as anything from persistent concern to overwhelming fear of imminent death. The fear and apprehension emotions that are associated with all forms of anxiety are usually accompanied by a number of characteristic physical and physiological symptoms. People who experience anxiety to the extent that it is disabling, or at least disrupting their life, may suffer from one of several disorders. These are outlined below in 'Signs and symptoms'. It is also the case that anxiety can be a secondary part, or consequence, of physical illness (see Table 2.4.1) or can be the underlying cause of complaints that are presented somatically. Difficulties in coping with anxiety can lead to substance misuse (alcohol, prescribed medication and non-prescribed drugs).

Figure 2.4.1

The Yerkes–Dobson curve

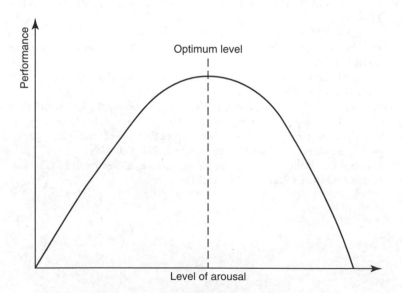

What is anxiety?
- Anxiety is a normal response to stress.
- Anxiety becomes problematic when it has a detrimental effect on the individual's ability to function.
- The key characteristic of anxiety problems is the prevailing feeling of apprehension, combined with physiological symptoms such as muscular tension, sweating, palpitations, dizziness and hyperventilation.

Signs and symptoms

Generalized anxiety disorder (GAD)

This is a generalized and relatively persisting (6+ months) feeling of excessive, problematic anxiety or worry about a situation or event. The individual presenting with the anxiety symptoms may not be able to identify the precise reasons for their anxiety at first. There may be a lot of worry and apprehension that the person is very much aware of and preoccupied with. The person may also feel tense, restless and fatigued, have sleep disturbance (usually sleep onset) and some of the other physical symptoms associated with panic attacks (see below). Additional psychological problems may include poor concentration, worrying, increased vigilance and irritability/intolerance.

Generalized anxiety can have a sudden onset and may only last for a short time before being resolved, or it can be a chronic problem that increases and decreases in severity but never quite goes away. Generalized anxiety can lead to, or co-exist with, other problems such as substance misuse, depression and more specific phobias.

Panic disorder

Panic disorder is characterized by short, intense and recurrent panic attacks. These are short bouts of overwhelming anxiety that occur suddenly, and have no predictable pattern or trigger. The intense feeling of fear is strongly associated with other uncomfortable physical symptoms. These can include one or more of the following:

- Palpitations
- Sweating/hot flushes
- Cold 'chills'
- Hyperventilation
- A pounding heart
- Dizziness
- Trembling
- Chest pain
- Choking sensation
- Nausea
- Stomach churning.

Panic attacks are usually short-lived episodes (a few minutes at most) in which the person is hyperaware of their psychological and physical symptoms. Panic disorder is diagnosed if the individual experiences three separate attacks in the absence of any objective danger over a 3-week period. The person should also be free of problematic anxiety in between the three attacks over this period. Panic disorder is diagnosed with reference to agoraphobia (that is, with or without agoraphobia). This is because it is felt that agoraphobia is based on a fear of having a panic attack in public and not being able to cope. It is important to rule out other possible physical illness-related causes of the symptoms (see below). People will often present their panic disorder in primary care settings in the form of a suspected heart or respiratory-related medical disorder (see nurse's role below). It is also the case that panic disorder often co-exists with depressive disorder, with up to 25% of people with panic disorder having a major depressive episode (Otto and Gould, 1996).

Panic attacks can lead the person to associate the situations in which their attacks have occurred with the unpleasant feelings they've experienced. This so-called 'anticipatory anxiety' may then lead to avoidance and the development of phobias; hence, the connection to agoraphobia.

Focused anxieties

These are otherwise known as phobias. They involve an unreasonable or unfounded fear of an object or situation and they usually lead to avoidance behaviours. There are three main types of phobia:

- *Specific/simple phobias* to objects or situations such as needles, blood, spiders and the dark. The fear can be to the object or situation itself but is more commonly to the anticipation or idea of the specific object or situation.
- *Social phobias* involving a fear of 'social performance' situations such as speaking or eating in public. The fear is usually of behaving in ways that are humiliating or embarrassing (being sick, fainting, being lost for words, shaking) in front of unfamiliar people who will judge the person by this behaviour.
- *Agoraphobia* involving fears about being in places or situations where escape may be difficult or help may not be available should the person have a panic attack.

People develop phobias to all sorts of situations but these commonly include being in a crowd, in a shopping centre/large store, being on a train or bus and generally being outside of the person's home.

Obsessive compulsive disorder (OCD)

Obsessions are recurrent, intrusive and unwanted thoughts or mental images (not hallucinations), which the person finds distressing. The thoughts or images persist despite attempts to block them out and despite the person being aware that they are often absurd. Obsessions often include unpleasant thoughts about violence, contamination (most common), blasphemy and sex. The key characteristics are the repetitive, unpleasant and unwanted nature of the thoughts.

Compulsions are repetitive acts that are usually performed in response to an obsession. Classically, they include washing to remain or become clean, checking the whereabouts and safety of knives or gas appliances, or arranging objects in particular ways to achieve order/symmetry. Compulsive behaviour is usually based on precise rules and has a ritual quality about it. The aim is to reduce discomfort from the obsessive thoughts or prevent a feared event from occurring, though the act is not usually an effective or objectively reasonable way of dealing with the thoughts. Obsessive–compulsive disorder is therefore based on the existence of, and attempt to manage, excessive anxiety. Resisting the obsessive thoughts or not carrying out the compulsive acts will increase the level of anxiety experienced.

OCD is diagnosed where the obsessions and compulsions interfere with the person's ability to function and take up more than an hour of their day. OCD tends to lead to avoidance of possible trigger situations or stimuli and can lead to depression and substance misuse as a coping strategy. Males and females tend to be equally affected, with onset being in teenage years. Most people who develop OCD have a pre-existing obsessive personality type.

Prognosis

Generalized anxiety disorder: GAD is difficult to diagnose and by definition involves experience of symptoms over a relatively long period. However, the problematic effects of generalized anxiety can occur suddenly and last for a short period or can wax and wane as a chronic problem.
Panic disorder: age of onset appears to be linked to prognosis. Earlier onset often results in a chronic course and poorer prognosis, though symptoms wax and wane over time. Later onset (especially after age 55) has a more optimistic prognosis with symptoms also appearing to be less severe.

OCD: tends to be chronic with on-going variations in severity of symptoms. People with obsessions only and maintaining factors such as persistent life stresses and pre-existing personality have a poorer prognosis.

Incidence and distribution

Generalized anxiety disorder has a reported prevalence rate of 6–7% in the general population. The population prevalence of panic disorder is approximately 1–2% (Horwath and Weissmann, 1997). Obsessive–compulsive disorder has a population prevalence of approximately 1–2% (Greist, 1995). Anxiety *symptoms* are much more common than anxiety disorders. Anxiety disorders tend to be more prevalent in the younger (20s/30s) age groups with older people (40+) tending to have co-existing depressive disorder.

Cause(s)

There is a variety of possible underlying causes of anxiety disorders. The stress–vulnerability model of predisposing, precipitating and maintaining factors is a useful way of organizing thinking about these.

Biological factors

Biological factors that may predispose some individuals to anxiety disorders include genetic inheritance of personality and temperament characteristics and dysfunction of autonomic nervous system where there are parasympathetic abnormalities. There is less evidence for genetic predisposition in generalized anxiety and panic disorders than in OCD or depressive disorders. There is strong evidence that OCD involves an overactive circuit between the pre-frontal cortex of the brain and the basal ganglia. Biochemical abnormalities in the seratonin system are also thought to play a part in this. There is also evidence of a genetic contribution with up to 50% of OCD presenters having a family history of similar symptoms.

Physical illnesses

The symptoms of anxiety disorders are a common feature of a number of physical diseases. In such situations anxiety is a secondary problem resulting from the primary physical illness. Differential diagnosis should rule out the conditions in Table 2.4.1 below.

Learned behaviour

It is important to avoid blaming the person for their anxiety symptoms. However, learned behaviour may be a cause of some people's anxiety symptoms, especially where they have learnt to fear objects or situations during their early years and have received inappropriate emotional reinforcement of these fears. It is also possible that some people learn maladaptive thinking and coping patterns (such as catastrophizing and

Table 2.4.1

Symptoms of anxiety disorders common to physical illness

Endocrine disorder	Thyrotoxicosis/hyperthyroidism Parathyroid disease Phaeochromocytoma Carcinoid syndrome
Diabetes	Hypoglaecemia
Brain disorder	Temporal lobe epilepsy (OCD) Head injury Tourette's syndrome (OCD)
Substance use/misuse	Drug and alcohol withdrawal Drugs misuse – marijuana, amphetamines Cold remedies containing pseudoephedrine Excessive drinking of caffeine
Mental illness	Depression Schizophrenia Anorexia nervosa (OCD) Dementia (OCD)

predicting danger) from parents or other close relatives and employ these when they feel stressed. A behavioural explanation of compulsions is that they are learned behaviours that are strengthened by the fact that anxiety reduction follows the compulsive act. This relief of anxiety symptoms makes it more likely that the act will be repeated in future when anxiety levels become uncomfortable again. Cognitive and behavioural therapies are effective ways of addressing such learned responses.

Stress reactions/life events

Stressful life events and the experience of psychological trauma are likely to provoke significant anxiety symptoms. The enduring nature of such symptoms may be due to learned and then generalized associations between the event and other similar situations. People faced by parental, partner or personally imposed demands for high achievement and excessive conformity are highly likely to experience high stress levels. Assessment of anxiety should always explore the existence or possibility of recent stressful life events or trauma experiences.

Relationship factors

Relationship factors such as separation anxiety in childhood and traumatic experiences of 'loss' or recent separations can act as both a predisposing and precipitating factor in anxiety disorders. OCD is thought by some to be a defensive regression to an earlier stage of development. Psychoanalytic explanations of anxiety claim that it is the result of unconscious psychological conflicts and the repression of deeply felt but unexpressed thoughts and feelings.

What causes anxiety disorder?
- Anxiety is caused by stress.
- People who develop problematic levels of anxiety may be predisposed to this by genetic inheritance, learned behaviour or maladaptive coping.
- Anxiety states can be precipitated by physical illness, substance misuse and stress that results from traumatic life events or relationship problems.

◄ *Key points*

Treatment of anxiety disorders

A range of interventions can be used to treat the symptoms of anxiety.

Medication

Medication has long been the most common form of treatment of anxiety disorders in primary care. Benzodiazepines (minor tranquillizers) have been the drug of choice for prescribing GPs. However, there is now much greater awareness of the dependence problems that benzodiazepines lead to when prescribed over long periods. Benzodiazepines also have considerable abuse potential and a 'street value'. Panic disorder symptoms tend to respond well to anti-depressant medication, especially tricyclics and SSRIs. Neither of these has the same dependency or abuse problems associated with benzodiazepines.

Social and emotional support

Simple forms of social and emotional support that provide the person with reassurance and a sense of psychological security can be a very effective way of responding to and reducing milder symptoms of general anxiety.

Talking therapies

Cognitive behaviour therapy (CBT) is the most effective form of psychotherapy for generalised anxiety and panic disorders. CBT involves critically examining and challenging the beliefs that lead to fear and apprehension, rehearsal of anxiety-provoking situations, and behavioural testing of irrational beliefs. CBT should be carried out by a trained and qualified specialist. *Psychodynamic psychotherapy* is another form of specialist psychotherapy. It is insight orientated and involves the person exploring the inner and early relationship conflicts that may have led to or be maintaining anxiety-based responses.

Complementary therapies

Therapies such as *acupuncture*, *homeopathy*, *herbalism* and *massage* are popular but are not widely available on the NHS. They all have a relaxation and calming value if the patient believes in their efficacy. Specific r*elaxation techniques*, such as progressive muscle relaxation and co-ordinated deep breathing (PMR) can be learnt relatively easily and help to adjust breathing and release muscular tension.

Key points ➤

> **What can be done?**
> - Anxiety states respond well to simple supportive counselling and listening.
> - CBT is the most effective form of talking therapy for general anxiety and panic disorder.
> - Phobias and OCD can be treated effectively by behaviour therapy that uses graded exposure strategies.
> - Relaxation techniques and complementary therapies such as acupuncture, massage and meditation can all help to reduce anxiety levels.

The role of the primary health care nurse

Information-giving

The majority of people who experience anxiety disorders seek help and are treated in primary health care settings. Anxiety-based problems are often first presented as physical illnesses. Many of the symptoms of anxiety do, in fact, overlap with non-psychiatric medical disorders (irregular heart rate, muscular tension, hyperventilation) making identification and assessment difficult. Additionally, patients who have significant worries about their physical health because of the apparently physical symptoms that they have are often reluctant to accept a psychological explanation and continue to believe that they may have an undiagnosed illness. It is very important that possible physical causes are properly assessed and ruled out and the patient given test results and assessment findings before a psychological account of the symptoms is offered. Failure to do so leaves the possibility of physical illness open and will prolong the person's distress. While the GP has an obvious role in exploring differential diagnoses other members of the team, such as practice nurses, also have a part to play in ensuring that the patient is clearly and fully informed about investigations and results.

Education
Explanation of the fight–flight response and of the physiological basis of many of the symptoms of anxiety can help patients to normalize their experiences and reduce their worries about underlying health problems. Primary health care nurses should also be in a good position to offer simple instruction on relaxation (PMR) techniques and should be able to give advice or referral information on the local availability of talking and complementary therapies.

Supportive counselling and listening
As with depression, listening and basic relationship building can be an effective way of reducing some of the anxiety-related distress that people experience. Supportive counselling combined with some pragmatic problem-solving guidance, working out practical ways of coping with symptoms or stressful situations, is an effective way of enabling the patient to see their problems as being within their own sphere of influence and control.

Support groups, helplines and further information
Contact details and an explanation of the range of help and resources for each of the following organizations can be found in the 'A–Z of support groups' on pp. 134–154.

- First Steps to Freedom
- The Mental Health Foundation
- MIND
- National Phobics Society
- No Panic
- Royal College of Psychiatrists
- Triumph over Phobia (TOP UK).

CASE STUDY 2.4.1

Linda Travis is a 24-year-old woman who is training to be an accountant. She has recently become a regular attender at the surgery. She has complained of feeling short of breath and 'faint' while at work and when she goes out shopping. Linda feels that her GP isn't taking her worries seriously and has requested an appointment with the practice nurse 'to have a chat' about them. During conversation Linda complains that there must be something wrong with her as she has recently also experienced palpitations and chest pain and that this was 'real', even though the GP said he couldn't find anything wrong.

How would you respond to Linda's complaint that her GP never takes her seriously?

- Explore the nature of her dissatisfaction and find out her expectations of the GP.
- Explain the GP's medical diagnosis role and professional concern.
- Give information on the GP's current approach/thoughts on Linda's presentation.

How would you go about broaching the possible psychological nature of Linda's problems?

- Explain the differential diagnosis approach of GPs/medical practitioners, introducing the possibility that symptoms can be indicative of a wide range of conditions.
- Ask about/clarify Linda's explanation/worst fears.
- Explain how worries/concerns/distress can be expressed in a variety of ways, including real physical symptoms.
- Make the point that psychological ill-health is still 'real' and is of no lesser concern to staff than physical illness.

What could be done to help Linda overcome her current worries and fears?

- Normalize her experience/symptoms with explanation of anxiety response/physiological basis.
- Offer short-term supportive counselling.
- Discuss the possibility of specialist counselling/CBT referral.
- Give information on relaxation techniques and alternative therapies.

References

Greist, J.H. (1995). Apparent depression, hidden obsession: uncovering obsessive compulsive disorder. *Primary Care Psychiatry*, 2-A.

Horwath, B. and Weissman, M.M. (1997). Epidemiology of the anxiety disorders in cross cultural groups. In S. Freeman (Ed.) *Cultural Issues in the Treatment of Anxiety*. New York: Guildford Press.

Otto, M. and Gould, R.A. (1996). Maximizing treatment outcome for panic disorder, cognitive behavioural strategies. In M.H. Pollack, M.W. Otto and J.F. Rosenbaum (Eds.) *Challenges in Clinical Practice: Pharmacologic and Psychosocial Strategies*. New York: Guildford Press.

2.5   SUBSTANCE MISUSE AND ADDICTIONS

Definitions

Most people who use and even abuse alcohol or drugs do not become addicts, and many come to no harm, although for some it may still create problems in their lives.

Use of alcohol is a legal and generally a socially acceptable activity. Use of illicit drugs is illegal, but may well be viewed as acceptable within certain sub-groups of people; indeed, there may be group pressure to join in with drinking and/or drug taking.

. . . so often does a drug follow the route from wonder cure to deadly fix . . .

Street Drugs, Andrew Tyler (1988)

Misuse of prescribed drugs, such as analgesia, tranquillizers and night sedation, often begins with legitimate use to alleviate symptoms, but slides into use for the effect of the drug alone, regardless of any symptomatic relief. In such circumstances it is seldom a group activity and the sufferer usually goes to great lengths to hide their habit and to deny any addiction. However, some prescription drugs do have a street value and are sold on the black market to those who abuse other drugs.

Volatile substance abuse (VSA), including solvents – so-called 'glue-sniffing' – occurs mainly in groups of pre-teens and young teenagers. The substances are not illegal in themselves but it is an offence to supply anyone under the age of 18 with a substance that one suspects will be taken to achieve intoxication.

Incidence and distribution

Misuse of and addiction to alcohol, drugs and volatile substances is prevalent worldwide. It can be traced back to earliest history and persists despite legislation, taxation, health scares and education about the physical, psychological and social damage it may cause. Numbers are calculated by general population survey, measuring substance-related disease incidence and attendance at rehabilitation projects, but it is believed to be vastly under-estimated and under-diagnosed. Certain countries (USA, UK, France, Italy, Russia) have a higher incidence of alcohol problems and cultures within these show increased prevalence (Scots, Irish, Native Americans, Australian/New Zealand indigenous groups), whereas other cultural groups have a lower than average incidence (Jews, Chinese and Japanese). It is more commonly a problem for men.

Causes

A number of factors are implicated in substance misuse, which may not be causal but probably increase vulnerability to dependence or perpetuate addictive behaviour.

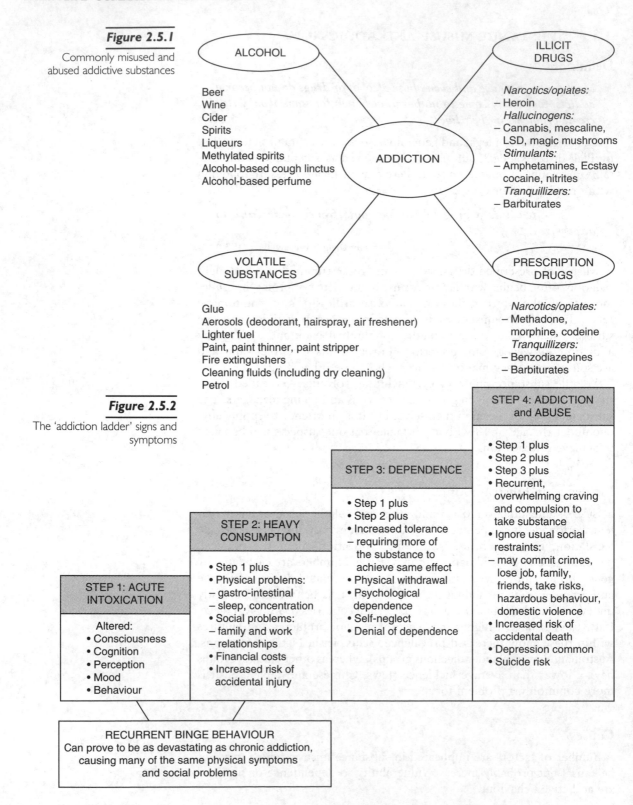

Figure 2.5.1

Commonly misused and abused addictive substances

Figure 2.5.2

The 'addiction ladder' signs and symptoms

Genetic

Alcoholism appears to run in families. This can also be explained by living in an environment where drink and drunkenness are overt. However, twin and adoptive studies indicate that genetic inheritance does play a part.

Learned behaviour

This relates to the environmental influences around, especially those experienced from an early age, but also to learned behaviour that informs the individual that drinking or drug taking alleviates anxiety in the short-term and in the long-term the problems it begets can be obliterated by further drink or drugs.

Biology

Studies identify biological make-up, which makes addiction in an individual more likely, but evidence is not conclusive. Some individuals seem predisposed to develop psychotic symptoms under the influence of alcohol and certain drugs.

Personality

Suggestions of an addictive type of personality have never been adequately scientifically demonstrated, but it persists as an unsubstantiated theory.

Peer-group pressure

Certain youth cultures seduce young people into substance abuse, where it is 'cool' to join in and to abstain is to miss out on the group experience. Older generations also demonstrate peer group pressure, of the, 'Come on, have another drink' variety.

Social deprivation

Alcohol and drugs appear to offer some escape from the hardships of life. Where there is unemployment and an empty day ahead the pub provides an alternative venue to home and drink and drugs can alleviate the boredom. Of course, the expense leads to further social deprivation.

Extreme stress

Stress and distress can lead to excessive use of drink and drugs and addiction compounds problems, but increased use provides a further escape route, and so the vicious circle is complete.

High-risk occupation

Certain occupations carry a higher risk of alcohol-related problems (pub-work, catering, brewing, distilling, journalism, armed forces, doctors). Illicit drug use is expensive and the image of drugs being the playground of the rich and famous still holds truth. However, *anyone* can become addicted and where money is scarce, addiction often leads to crime to support a drug habit.

Key points ➤

> **Causes of substance misuse and addiction**
> - Genetic
> - Learned behaviour
> - Biology
> - Personality
> - Peer-group pressure
> - Social deprivation
> - Extreme stress
> - High-risk occupation.

Street slang for drugs and drug behaviours

As well as the proper names for prescribed and illicit drugs there are a number of slang terms, of which it is useful to be aware. The class of the drug dictates the seriousness of the penalty. A Class B drug prepared for injection automatically rises to Class A status.

Table 2.5.1

Classification of drugs and methods of use

Drug and class	Routes	Slang terms
Amphetamines: Class B	Orally, as pills or powders	Speed, uppers, pep-pills, whiz
Nitrates: amyl/butyl	Sniffed direct or via soaked rag	Poppers, snappers, rush
Cocaine	Sniffed via a straw/bank note ('snorting') Heated to purify and sniffed ('free-basing' – v. potent) Eaten, chewed, ball (absorbed via genitalia) Intravenously	Coke, snow, a line, Charlie, 'C' Crack (sound made as heated) Rocks, stones
Ecstasy: Class A	Orally as pills, often at 'rave' parties and gigs	'E', 'XTC', doves, Eve, Edward
Barbiturates: Class C Benzodiazepines	Orally as pills Intramuscularly and intravenously	Downers, barbs, sleepers Mandies, tranks (x), sekkies
Cannabis: Class B	Inhalation of hemp plant leaves or resin mixed with tobacco in the form of a roll-up – 'joint', 'spliff', 'reefer' Via a clay pipe or hookah Eaten, usually as a cake	Hemp, marijuana, weed, herb, ganja, hash(ish), blow, grass Pot, dope, shit, rope, skunk
Heroin: Class A	Snorted, smoked Heated and inhaled, as in 'chasing the dragon' Intramuscularly and subcutaneously – skin popping Injected intravenously – 'main-lining', 'shooting up'	A fix, smack, 'H', junk, brown Horse, skag
LSD: Class A	Orally as pills and powder	PCP, angel dust, acid, trips, tabs, (micro)dots
Magic mushrooms (Psiocybins, amanita muscaria)	Eaten as fresh or dried mushrooms, may be mixed with food where mushrooms are a usual ingredient	Liberty cap, fly agaric
Solvents and volatile substances	Inhaled direct – 'sniffing' or from a plastic bag held over the nose	

Problems created by substance misuse

- The stress that is being avoided by the substance misuse is actually exacerbated by the dependence on drugs, alcohol or volatile substances.
- The behaviour of the misuser becomes unpredictable.
- Normal routines cannot be met and responsibilities kept, especially those related to employment.
- It causes arguments and even violence.
- Vulnerable family members, especially children, can be psychologically damaged by the neglect, abuse or disturbance incurred by the addiction.
- Channels of communication between family and friends will be disrupted.
- The whole family might become isolated as a result of the social effects of dependence.
- The craving for greater amounts of the substance may lead to debt and crime.

Associated conditions with alcohol, drug and solvent misuse

There are many hazards associated with substance misuse and minimization of harm is as important an issue to address as an attempt at total withdrawal. There is potential for harm from the effects and side-effects of the substance, the method by which it is taken and as a result of risky behaviour while under its influence.

> *The impact of a drug is not fixed. It depends on dose, expectations, the mental and physical condition of the user and the setting in which it is taken.*
>
> *Street Drugs*, Andrew Tyler (1988)

Young people and substance use and misuse

One of the main reasons given for the initial experimentation and continued use of alcohol, drugs or solvents is that it is a fun group activity creating social cohesion and a feeling of belonging among peers. There may also be a degree of peer group pressure to participate and fear of exclusion from the group may outweigh any trepidation about the dangers of experimentation. Another reason for the prevalence of substance misuse in young people is the escape it appears to offer from the stress of making the transition from youth to adulthood: this may be about family, relationships, school-work, exams and future employment. These life-events coincide with a time when great physical changes, particularly hormonal changes, are taking place and sexual identity may also be an issue. Good communication between adults and young people is vital in order to pass on the necessary information about alcohol, drugs and solvents: they will 'switch off' if they suspect adults are being patronizing, controlling, dictatorial, or out of touch with what it is to be young. There is also a clear need for the young person to be given time and emotional space to talk to adults who are prepared to listen and to be as non-judgmental as possible.

Table 2.5.2

Desired and actual effects of
substance misuse

Substance	Desired effects	Side-effects	Route-effects
Alcohol *Central nervous system depressant*, which gives the initial impression of being a stimulant. Rates of absorption differ between men (slower) and women (quicker) and according to body weight (the smaller and slighter, the faster absorbed). Absorption is slowed by food, especially bulky carbohydrates (bread, potatoes, pasta).	• Relaxation • Sleep inducing, social disinhibition • Initial elevation of mood • Suppression of unwanted thoughts/feelings • Health benefits (of certain types of alcohol taken at low levels) in protecting against coronary heart disease (for men aged 40+ and women post-menopause).	Hangover symptoms, gastro-intestinal tract (inflammation, bleeds, ulcers, vomiting, diarrhoea), appetite/weight (loss/gain), nutritional deprivation, poor sleep/concentration/memory, pancreatitis, hepatitis and cirrhosis of the liver, cancer (mouth, oesophagus, pharynx, larynx, breast, liver), reduced fertility (male and female), foetal-alcohol syndrome in pregnant women, peripheral neuropathy, cardiac and lung disease, black-outs, epileptic fits, alcoholic dementia including Korsakoff syndrome, severe withdrawal including delirium tremens (DTs), anxiety and depression, accidental injury and death (from impaired judgement, risky behaviour, hypothermia and choking on vomit, death by extreme intoxication)	The actual volume of liquid drunk, as well as its nature, make it more likely that vomiting will occur while the drinker is unconscious or semi-conscious, increasing the risk of inhalation and death
Stimulants *Central nervous system stimulant*: amphetamines, cocaine, ecstasy, nitrites (amyl nitrite, butyl nitrite)	Boosts energy/confidence/concentration/feeling of well-being, a rush of good feeling, which is at once physical and psychological, suppressed appetite, increased libido, enhanced sexual experience (although erogenous zones *less* responsive), increased diureses	Exhaustion, depression and anxiety, agitation and ill-temper, dehydration (excessive activity without replenishing fluids), tolerance quickly built up, psychosis (paranoid delusions and auditory hallucinations) – may trigger schizophrenia, exacerbation of medical conditions of heart, kidneys, eyes, blood pressure, endocrine system – sudden vascular dilatation and tachy-cardia causes cardiac arrest	Sniffing causes damage to mucous membrane of the nose
Hallucinogenics Cannabis,	Heightened perceptions, euphoria, relaxation ('mellowing out'), helps to alleviate muscle spasm symptoms for some multiple sclerosis, muscular dystrophy sufferers	Impaired functioning/apathy, cut-off and remote behaviour, hypersensitivity in some users – acute paranoid states, lowered sperm count (appears to be reversible), possibly carcino-genic, symptoms of psychosis – triggers schizophrenia, 'flash-backs', 'bad trip' results in self-inflicted harm, even death	Smoking: includes all the dangers of tobacco and nicotine inhalation
LSD, DMT,	'Mind-expanding' experiences: self-realization		
Magic mushrooms			Poisoning if mushroom species is wrongly identified

Table 2.5.2

(Continued)

Substance	Desired effects	Side-effects	Route-effects
Opiates Heroin	A rush of well-being (especially when injected); *however*, not usually taken to feel high, but rather to feel normal – the 'cotton wool' effect makes life bearable, relief from pain, relief from anxiety, dreamy, relaxed sensation, deadening of senses	Acute withdrawal: sweating, runny nose, increased diuresis, constipation, low respiration, low body temperature, weight loss, self-neglect, women suffer menstrual dysfunction but still ovulate – danger of pregnancy and birth of addicted baby, born with withdrawal symptoms	Intravenous injection: dirty needles causing inflamed, infected sites, thrombosed veins, circulatory problems, shared needles (HIV, AIDS, hepatitis), overly pure heroin (death with IV use), mixed ('cut') with unsuitable substances, accidental overdose
Barbiturates *Central nervous system depressant*: tuinal, nembutal, seconal, mandrax	Produce tranquillity, some drowsiness, but not analgesic, deadening of senses and physical powers, released inhibitions	Fine line between therapeutic and lethal dose, alcohol hangover symptoms, leaden numbness, increased tolerance, physical withdrawal (tremor, shakes, irritability, anxiety)	Often taken with alcohol, which increases effect and can result in accidental overdose and death
Tranquillizers Benzodiazipines, valium, librium	Induce sedation, produce tranquillity, allay anxiety	Tolerance develops easily, blurring of intellectual ability, effect increased with alcohol – potentially lethal combination	Some users mix with liquid and inject, causing local and systemic damage
Solvents and volatile substances	Initial euphoria, drowsiness, perceptual disturbance	Rash around nose and mouth, chronic cold symptoms, weight loss, arrhythmias, bronchial spasm, brain damage, aplastic anaemia, polyneuropathy, toxic effects can be fatal	Accidental suffocation, risky behaviour – accidental injury and death

Health education

There are different schools of thought about how explicit education on drugs, alcohol and VSA should be. The key debate is whether the information encourages and leads directly to experimentation or whether awareness of the potential dangers provide enough warning to discourage experimentation. The philosophy behind most voluntary and health education agencies advocates providing enough information for people to make informed choices. If they do then choose to drink, take drugs or sniff glue, the hope is that they have enough awareness to understand the very real risks and to minimize these. For example, if someone is determined to take ecstasy and go to an all-night rave, it is better that they understand

Figure 2.5.3

Consequences of substance abuse in young people

Young people and alcohol

- Parental attitudes to drinking have the greatest influence on the child's consumption
- Teetotal parents are more likely to rear teetotallers *or* heavy drinkers
- Most trouble is usually associated with binge drinking, not steady, regular consumption
- Heavy drinking is often an indicator of other high-risk behaviour, smoking, drugs, etc.
- Effects of alcohol have greater impact on the body due to lack of experience handling mood-altering substances
- Hangover symptoms, tiredness, poor concentration, lethargy and altered appetite are physical signs and symptoms to watch for
- Under-age drinking and subsequent high-risk behaviour can lead to truancy from school, unplanned pregnancy, law-breaking, violence, and accidents

Young people and VSA

- Signs of abuse:
  – appear drunk (not long-lasting)
  – chemical smell to breath/clothes
  – rash around mouth
  – empty aerosols around
  – household substances disappear or are used up fast
- Experimentation and continuing use often starts in the home
- Death can occur with the first experimentation
- Fatalities three times more likely than with illegal drugs
- Prolonged use can cause chronic damage to brain, liver and kidneys

Young people and drugs

- There may be heavy peer group pressure to experiment with drugs
- Drug taking is strongly linked with certain youth activities: it may be hard to resist drugs at a rave or club
- In the long-term affects physical well-being: lank hair, poor skin, weight loss, lethargy
- If young person unforthcoming about drug use check for needle marks – inner arm, behind knee
- Increasing money problems may be a sign
- Loss of interest in normally diverting activities, friends or hobbies may be a sign
- Missing spoons and/or discoloured spoons found in young person's room
- Tubs of vitamin C might be passed off as healthy, but used to shoot heroin

Figure 2.5.4

Approaching health education issues

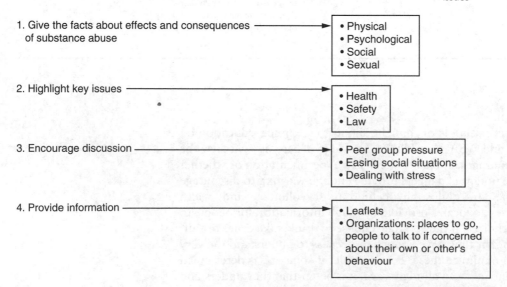

1. Give the facts about effects and consequences of substance abuse ⟶
- Physical
- Psychological
- Social
- Sexual

2. Highlight key issues ⟶
- Health
- Safety
- Law

3. Encourage discussion ⟶
- Peer group pressure
- Easing social situations
- Dealing with stress

4. Provide information ⟶
- Leaflets
- Organizations: places to go, people to talk to if concerned about their own or other's behaviour

Desired effects	Undesirable effects
Benzodiazipines work by blocking receptors that receive the body's messages that it is experiencing stress.	The normal response to stress is for the body to produce endorphins – a natural pain killer; however, the benzodiazipine-blocked messages halt the process of production.
The adrenaline reflex is slowed, producing a muted response to stress and danger.	'Adrenaline rebound' occurs where adrenaline is released in an uncontrolled way, unrelated to need, producing the sudden sensation of a panic attack.
The drugs are long-acting and long-lasting.	They are slow to leave the system and remain in the fat cells for months, making withdrawal a long, slow process.
The major effect of the drug is to provide short-term protection from the acute psychological pain of trauma.	Memory is dulled, concentration is reduced and the ability to take in and process information is interfered with: counselling and psychotherapy are of limited value due to this clouding of the mental faculties.

Table 2.5.3

Desired and undesirable effects of benzodiazipines

how crucial it is to drink plenty of fluids. Similarly, if they are taking IV drugs they need to know the risks of sharing needles and the measures to take to minimize cross-infection.

Dependence and addiction to prescribed drugs

These include anxiolytics, (minor) tranquillizers, sedatives, and night sedation.

The issue of tackling benzodiazipine dependence is complicated by the fact that this treatment was initially recommended as a therapeutic intervention for symptoms of anxiety, stress or insomnia. It is probably fair to say that in the short-term these medications can provide a useful barrier to some of the more severe symptoms, but when given long-term and necessarily in increasing doses they begin to exacerbate the symptoms. Indeed, doctors treating patients who repeatedly present with persisting and more severe symptoms of anxiety may well merely prescribe higher doses, thus perpetuating the problem. In addition, more is being learned about the symptoms of long-term benzodiazipine use and many of these symptoms are quite unusual and therefore not easily recognized as being related to the benzodiazipine dependence. A great deal of time and money may be spent investigating them as independent problems and treating them with a number of therapies, most of which to fail to help because the benzodiazipines continue to be taken. There is also a danger of the patient being labelled as difficult to treat, even hypochondriacal, and entrenched in their problems.

For the sufferer presenting for help to come off benzodiazipine treatment there may be:

- resentment towards the prescribing doctor
- confusion over why the treatment for anxiety is now causing the anxiety symptoms to be more acute
- loss of confidence in the expertise of the 'experts'.

Management and treatment of addiction

The starting point for management and treatment of addiction is twofold: firstly, the sufferer must acknowledge that they have a problem; secondly, they must accept responsibility for their own behaviour. The issue of taking responsibility is often central: people close to the sufferer often report their frustration at a denial of responsibility and a blaming of others and life-experiences for the addiction. There may well be a number of factors that have led to the addiction and there are methods of treatment and professional and voluntary agencies to lend expertise, help and support in kicking it. However, it is crucial for the sufferer to understand that *they* are ultimately the ones who are in control of changing their behaviour.

> *Success stories are not necessarily about people becoming drug-free. In some cases it's about those who have not resorted to crime for a year – perhaps the longest period they have managed in their adult lives.*

Sue Mapp (1998)

Management covers two main approaches: one of damage limitation where safer behaviour around the substance misuse is advocated, and the other of planned and monitored withdrawal and detoxification from the substance. The latter is most likely to be undertaken as an in-patient in a psychiatric hospital or specialist unit, certainly in the early stages when the physical side-effects of withdrawal can be severe and potentially threatening to health and even life. Sometimes a substitute for the addictive substance is prescribed, such as methadone in place of heroin. This in itself deserves mention, because misunderstanding abounds about this practice: *methadone is as equally addictive as heroin*. However, it is prescribed in order to remove the person from the criminal activity of buying (or stealing to buy) and using heroin, as well as giving them the opportunity to step away from the powerful social culture of heroin addiction, while also providing medical supervision of their habit and controlled withdrawal if this is desired.

Addiction and the role of the primary health care nurse

The primary health care nurse may well have a constant but changing role in the care of someone with an addiction.

Detection and recognition of the early warning signs of substance misuse

Sufferers of an addiction may present with physical symptoms related to their addiction, or indeed social, psychological, personal and relationship difficulties. The substance misuse may not represent an addiction, but if it causes problems for the sufferer it will certainly need tackling. The fact that the person is presenting for help suggests there is some self-recognition of a need for help. It is important not to put the person off, so sensitive probing is required, but there is equally a need for a straightforward and

Advice for withdrawal
- Don't go it alone.
- Do it under medical advice.
- Don't stop medication suddenly: there may be a danger of fitting.
- Transfer to a long-acting benzodiazipine, such as valium, is recommended: it is produced in a number of doses down to 2 mg, which is scored and can be halved to 1 mg, making for a gentler withdrawal process.
- Recommended withdrawal rate is 1 mg per fortnight – recovery may take a year or more.
- The 'patient' needs to be in control of their own recovery.
- Self-help groups and voluntary organizations may be invaluable.
- Cognitive behavioural therapy may be of benefit.
- The patient may have been in denial for a long time: denying the severity of the problem to themselves, perhaps upping the prescribed dose and signing on with more than one GP to gain extra prescriptions, and perhaps behaving secretively to hide their addiction from friends, family and work colleagues.
- Support will be needed to help them claim back their lives.

matter-of-fact approach in order to identify the nature and extent of the problem. It may be a friend or relative who presents to the primary health care nurse, in which case the aim is to provide information and support that helps them to persuade the sufferer to establish direct contact with health services. Give-away symptoms include changes in mood and behaviour, including sleep pattern, inability to maintain the usual commitments to school-work, job or home, and physical frailty and deterioration in health condition (hair, skin, nails), needle marks (IV drug use), or a rash around mouth (solvents).

Figure 2.5.5

Withdrawal symptoms

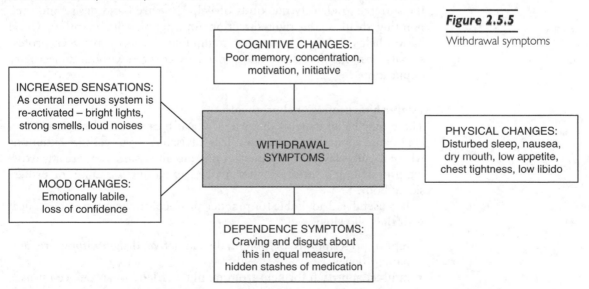

COGNITIVE CHANGES:
Poor memory, concentration, motivation, initiative

INCREASED SENSATIONS:
As central nervous system is re-activated – bright lights, strong smells, loud noises

WITHDRAWAL SYMPTOMS

PHYSICAL CHANGES:
Disturbed sleep, nausea, dry mouth, low appetite, chest tightness, low libido

MOOD CHANGES:
Emotionally labile, loss of confidence

DEPENDENCE SYMPTOMS:
Craving and disgust about this in equal measure, hidden stashes of medication

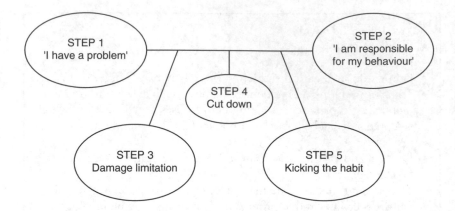

Figure 2.5.6

Management and treatment of addiction

Assessment of core and associated problems

Use of a formal assessment questionnaire may be most useful in elucidating pertinent information (see Section 3.1, 'Patient Assessment'). This helps to reduce any embarrassment over the personal nature of the questions and ensures that all the necessary points are covered. Understandably, there may be great resistance from the patient who fears being labelled 'alcoholic', 'drug addict' or 'glue-sniffer'. Less formal questioning is also useful in opening up more of a general dialogue between patient and nurse, which helps to promote a therapeutic relationship. Physical tests (urine, blood) can be carried out to screen for evidence of current drug and alcohol status, but require the patient's consent.

Appropriate referral and liaison

Awareness of the different types of help available is useful, but knowing how to find out this information is crucial. Time should be spent helping the sufferer to identify the kinds of help they need and desire and then pointing them in the right direction for specialist intervention. Good liaison helps to keep channels of communication open between professionals, ensuring that all aspects of need are covered without unnecessary duplication.

Establishing professional protocols

There may be an issue of the primary health care nurse being used as a confidante about illegal activities. It is advisable not to get into situations where legality clashes with patient confidentiality issues. Refer to any existing protocols and seek specialist advice from a nursing union or professional body.

It is useful and advisable for practice protocols to be established to deal with the following:

- repeat prescriptions of potentially addictive drugs without regular patient review
- indirect approach for help from family or friend of substance misuser

- management of patients presenting while acutely intoxicated by substances
- awareness of illegal activity related to substance misuse and addiction
- treatment of those under 16 years who do not wish parents to be informed
- the care of children in the responsibility of acutely intoxicated patient.

Assistance with this process can be sought from specialist agencies who are up to date with current trends in approaches to treatment.

Provision of education and resources

This may be practical in nature (e.g. information about needle exchange programmes) or may require more in-depth counselling (e.g. safer sexual practices, safer drug use). Primary health care nurses can play a key role in providing health education information, which prevents substance misuse in the first place. This may be through work with groups within the local community and may cover a broad range of topics (such as acceptable alcohol intake, the health risks associated with substance abuse).

On-going psychological support of sufferer and family members

The therapeutic relationship between carer and sufferer is often identified as pivotal in the eventual outcome of treatment for substance abuse and addiction: it is worth investing time in it. The primary health care nurse may be a carer to the carer and this is an equally important role. Professionals who work in the substance misuse and addiction field often emphasize the importance of keeping clear boundaries within the relationship where patient responsibility for their actions is understood. Some draw up contracts for behaviour (which may require in-depth discussion and negotiation) where both parties sign the agreement.

Supporting the 'supporters'

If someone presents to the primary health care nurse with concerns about a friend or relative's dependence on alcohol, drugs or volatile substances, there may be a number of ways in which they can be helped and supported:

- They may just need you to listen.
- They may need confirmation from you that there is, indeed, a dependence problem.
- They may need factual information about addiction, about the substance, etc.
- They may wish to be informed about available resources, local and national organizations etc.
- They may need referral to professional agencies, such as social services.
- They may actually be asking (in a roundabout way) for support for themselves.
- This support may need to be regular and on-going over months or years.

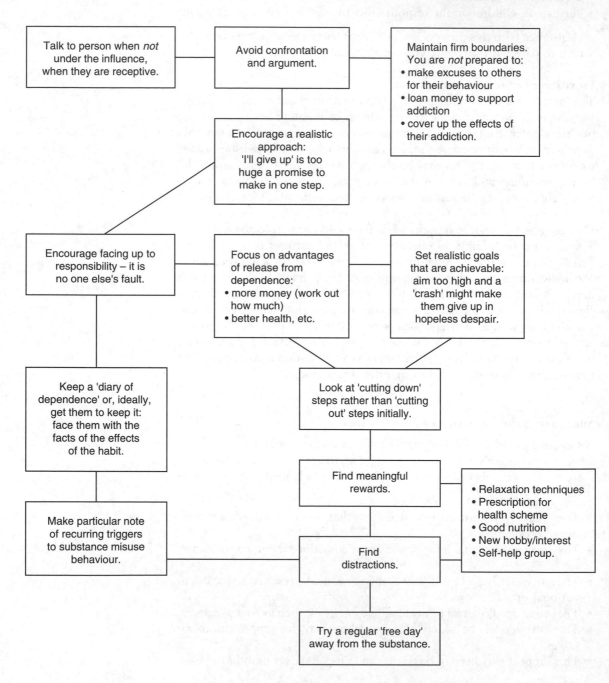

Figure 2.5.7

Advice for those supporting someone who is tackling substance misuse and withdrawal

The role of the primary health care nurse
- Recognition of the early warning signs of substance misuse.
- Identifying addiction with the patient.
- Assessment of core and associated problems.
- Appropriate referral and liaison.
- Providing education.
- Providing resources.
- On-going psychological support of sufferer and family members.

Support groups, helplines and further information

Contact details and an explanation of the range of help and resources for each of the following organizations can be found in the 'A–Z of support groups' on pp. 134–154.

- Adfam National
- African Caribbean Mental Health Association
- Al-Anon Family Groups UK and Eire
- Alcoholics Anonymous
- Alcohol Concern
- Counsel for Involuntary Tranquillizer Addiction (CITA)
- Drinkline
- GamCare
- The Institute for the Study of Drug Dependence
- The Mental Health Foundation
- MIND
- Release
- Re-Solv
- Scottish Council on Alcohol.

CASE STUDY 2.5.1

The occupational health nurse for a large department store is approached by an employee for advice about withdrawing from tranquillizers. The woman has been taking lorazepam for 3 years since the traumatic break-up of her marriage, but she has begun a new and important relationship and wants to finish with the medication. She finds her own GP less than helpful – he put her on the stuff in the first place and has been happy to repeat the prescription since – but she fears 'going it alone' without any professional support.

If you were that occupational health nurse how would you respond to this request?

- Welcome her request – be encouraging about her positive decision, while emphasizing that she may indeed have a tough journey ahead.
- Be honest and clear about your experience and ability to help – what you can and can't offer.
- Give your opinion about who she needs around her to support her through this time: suggest that she considers changing her GP to someone she can better relate to, discuss whether she will tell her new 'partner', find out if she has family and friends who know, and discuss whether she feels able to confide in her immediate boss.

What are the various areas in which you could offer help?

• Give her specific information about the effects of withdrawal physically and emotionally.
• Inform her that experts advise transfer to a long-acting drug such as valium, which can be reduced more gradually.
• Ask whether she has stashes of lorazepam around and offer to dispose of it safely.
• Identify specialist resources: voluntary organizations and specialist reading matter.
• Help her to learn relaxation techniques and self-help ways to deal with panic attacks.
• Give her advice about a healthy diet and lifestyle.
• Liaise (if requested) with her GP and her boss (especially about the ways in which withdrawal might impact on her work performance).
• Offer a regular slot every week to come and talk and offer to talk with her partner too, if desired.

CASE STUDY 2.5.2

A school nurse who has regular contact with a primary school for routine development and vaccination screenings has been asked to make a health promotion presentation about the dangers of drugs, alcohol and cigarettes to the oldest class, who are aged between 11 and 12.

How should she prepare for this?

• Consider her audience – age, likely knowledge base, depth and extent of information required.
• Presentation skills – involve children actively: brainstorm, report own experience (self, peers, parents), role-play, quiz.

Are there any special considerations to bear in mind?

• Age of the children – they are minors and some will be less 'street-wise' than others.
• Awareness of issues:
  – the tension between providing information that may deter or encourage experimentation
  – the argument that if they are going to experiment anyway, it is better that they know how best to stay safe.
• Parental approval/disapproval: consider a session where adults also attend with their child.
• Meet with school head and class teacher to discuss these issues and to go over material beforehand.
• Consider a letter home to inform parents prior to the session.

What resources might she draw on?

• Voluntary organizations – ask for free handouts.
• A reformed drug-user/alcoholic to attend with you to relate experiences and bear witness to the downside of these lifestyles.

References

Mapp, S. (1998). Drug dependency. *Practice Nurse*, 15.
Tyler, A. *Street Drugs*. London: Hodder & Stoughton.

2.6   DELIBERATE SELF-HARM AND SUICIDE

Definitions

The topic of deliberate self-harm (also referred to as 'parasuicide') can stir up difficult feelings, some of which we may not be aware of, or only half aware of, until we are faced with a specific situation. This can complicate the process of caring for someone who deliberately self-harms; for close relatives and friends, but also for the professional carer. It can be useful to view self-harm along a continuum and considered in this way it becomes clear that many of us carry out self-harming behaviour to a certain degree at certain times in our life, particularly in times of stress. Death by suicide at one end of the self-harm continuum is obviously the most extreme outcome, but at the other end we can include such behaviours as smoking despite the known health effects, drinking alcohol to excess, over-eating or eating over-processed foods, and so on down the hierarchy of behaviours.

Figure 2.6.1

Deliberate self-harm

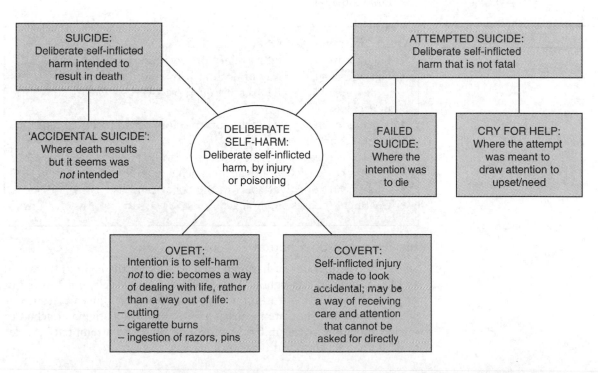

SUICIDE:
Deliberate self-inflicted harm intended to result in death

ATTEMPTED SUICIDE:
Deliberate self-inflicted harm that is not fatal

'ACCIDENTAL SUICIDE':
Where death results but it seems was *not* intended

DELIBERATE SELF-HARM:
Deliberate self-inflicted harm, by injury or poisoning

FAILED SUICIDE:
Where the intention was to die

CRY FOR HELP:
Where the attempt was meant to draw attention to upset/need

OVERT:
Intention is to self-harm *not* to die: becomes a way of dealing with life, rather than a way out of life:
– cutting
– cigarette burns
– ingestion of razors, pins

COVERT:
Self-inflicted injury made to look accidental; may be a way of receiving care and attention that cannot be asked for directly

Overt and covert self-harm

Overt and covert self-harm is very different from attempted suicide: the intention is to inflict injury and pain on the body and this behaviour usually becomes a way of dealing with and surviving emotional pain. Self-injury of this type is more widespread than is generally realized – many sufferers maintain high-powered and fruitful careers and home life – and it is far more common among women. The self-inflicted injury may be an external representation of inner, hidden, emotional injury and provide a physical focus for the emotional pain; as some sufferers have expressed, ' putting the pain outside where it is easier to cope with'. Equally it may be a way of expressing anger without hurting anyone else and many express a feeling of relief from tension when the injury has been inflicted. It can be a way of alerting others to inner pain and asking for help. Whatever the cause, the injury is saying something about the person' s life and a positive first step in dealing with self-injurious behaviour of this type is to ask and talk about it. Many sufferers express feelings of guilt and shame about their behaviour and the physical scars from their injuries can be a continuing reminder, which torments them. There can also be something addictive in nature about the compulsion to continue to repeat self-injurious behaviour. A common pattern is to self-injure, experience some relief from inner tension, but feel guilt and self-loathing and vow to stop this behaviour in future, but then a build-up of inner tension increases and, given certain entrenched triggers, such as stress, ultimately the self-injurious behaviour is repeated. Certainly treatment often needs to focus on breaking out of the pattern and finding alternative ways of expressing inner hurt (see Table 2.6.1, p. 78).

Key points ➤

> **Overt and covert self-harm**
> - The intention is to inflict injury on the body, but *not* to die.
> - The behaviour is a way of dealing with emotional pain.
> - It may be overt – obvious self-injury, or covert – made to look like an accident.
> - It provides a physical focus for emotional pain, relieves tension, expresses anger.
> - It may be a way of getting attention and help.
> - Sufferers often feel guilty at their behaviour.
> - There is an addictive aspect to the behaviour.
> - Treatment focuses on finding alternative ways to express inner hurt.

Incidence and distribution

Suicide and deliberate self-harming behaviour occur throughout the world and have done so throughout history. Rates vary widely, but this is not surprising, considering it is not always clear whether injury or death was by accidental or deliberate means. There is also still a stigma attached to suicide and some cover-up by those around might be attempted in order to mask the fact that death was by suicide.

In Britain, suicide accounts for about 1% of all deaths. Men are more likely to actually kill themselves, but women are more likely to attempt suicide: this difference may occur because men tend to choose a more violent and dangerous weapon, such as a gun. Young women (ages 15–19) are at greatest risk of attempting suicide. There is a higher incidence in the older age group (ages 50–60), although the rate in young men (ages 15–25) is currently showing the fastest increase. Rates are also higher amongst the single, divorced, or widowed. There are clear seasonal differences in suicide rates, a peak occurring in late winter and early spring.

◄ Key points

Incidence and distribution
- Occurs throughout the world and throughout history.
- Rates vary widely, partly due to differing ways of assessing whether death is by suicide.
- About 1% of all deaths in the UK is by suicide.
- Men are more likely to kill themselves than women.
- Women are more likely to attempt suicide.
- Rates are highest in the 50–60 age group.
- The sharpest rise is currently in young men.
- There are higher rates amongst the single, divorced, or widowed.
- Seasonal differences show a peak in late winter/early spring.

Causes: vulnerability factors

It is not always clear why someone decides to commit suicide, or indeed to deliberately harm themselves. Often there are a number of factors; perhaps a culmination of problems. When assessing risk from self-harm and suicide it is useful to consider a number of factors, which appear to make the individual more vulnerable to this behaviour.

Suffering from a mental illness

Someone with a known psychiatric disorder and history of mental health problems is at much greater risk of deliberate self-harm and suicide. Depression, particularly in the older age group, accounts for the greatest percentage of this vulnerable group. Those taking prescription medication for a mental health problem or those who have an illicit drug problem have ready access to the means to harm or kill themselves by overdosing. For those with an alcohol problem, the effect of the drink may well cloud any ability to prevent them acting on an impulse to self-harm.

History of self-injury and suicide attempts

There is a common fallacy around that those who threaten suicide as a 'cry for help' are unlikely to actually kill themselves: the truth is that *the majority of people who finally commit suicide made previous suicide attempts and had expressed their intentions to kill themselves beforehand.* Those who have a family member who has committed suicide are also at a much greater risk of self-harm and suicide.

Suffering from a chronic physical illness or disability

Knowledge of terminal illness or a chronic debilitating condition incurring loss of function and pain can become the motivating factors for committing suicide. This may be a reasoned decision taken by an individual who wishes to be in control of the manner of their dying. It is a controversial issue, much debated in the media, where concerned relatives, doctors and nurses have been found to have played a part in the process and have had to face the consequences of whether they aided death illegally or behaved with the compassion expected of a caring profession. It may equally be a decision taken in great fear before understanding the support that might have been available to help them come to terms with their condition and its consequences.

Social isolation

Connectedness to others through relationships seems to afford some protection against the risk of deliberate self-harm. These relationships need not necessarily be of great depth or meaning, but just provide enough contact to provide some sense of group identity and to temper behaviour.

Relationship difficulties

In young people this is often experienced with parents, whereas in adults this is most commonly with partners. When a close and significant relationship breaks down the consequences can feel devastating and the disorienting effect of the loss can provide a trigger for deliberate self-harm as an escape from distress. It is sometimes suggested that it also provides a method of revenge by making the other person feel guilty and responsible and can be used as a method to emotionally blackmail them back into continuing the relationship. However, such motivations cannot be assumed and exploration of them is most suitably the province of the trained counsellor and psychotherapist.

Major life event involving loss and humiliation: personal, financial, status, role

Bereavement and grieving are times of greater vulnerability. Similarly, acute feelings of loss can also be experienced on retirement or unemployment, with the subsequent disorientation of losing role, status and financial standing.

Self-identity crisis

This can be termed as the 'Who am I? uncertainty', which is particularly intense for young people developing into adult maturity and which might include confusion over sexuality and sexual identity. This can lead directly to low self-esteem.

There may be as many causes of low self-esteem as there are people who suffer from it. Feeling worthless and insignificant may provoke a desire to punish oneself by inflicting hurt, or extend to a desire to wipe that self out permanently. Low self-esteem may be a significant sign of an underlying depression.

Deliberate self-harm: vulnerability factors
- Suffering from a mental illness
- History of self-injury and suicide attempts
- Family history of self-injury and suicide attempts
- Suffering from a chronic physical illness or disability
- Social isolation
- Relationship problems
- Major life event involving loss: personal, employment, financial, status, role
- Self-identity crisis and low self-esteem.

Treatment and management

All too frequently health professionals have tended to dismiss those who self-harm and attempt suicide as time-wasters and to withhold attention from them. Viewed as deflecting attention from those who are really ill, 'through no fault of their own', they are therefore seen as less deserving of time, care and resources.

- To harm oneself is usually a sign of desperate inner emotional pain and suffering.
- It requires acceptance, acknowledgement, professional caring and urgent treatment.
- Treatment and management need to encompass a number of components: physical safety, feelings, thoughts and behaviour.

Physical safety

In the acute stage when there is high risk of deliberate self-harm and suicide the individual may require emergency admission to psychiatric hospital – if necessary under section of the Mental Health Act. While waiting for an ambulance or emergency psychiatric assessment to be arranged, the patient may require one-to-one constant supervision, which includes accompanying to the toilet. Potentially harmful objects, including clothing, such as scarves, belts or neckties, may need to be removed. The carer also needs to be aware of proximity to glass doors or windows and drinks given in glasses or crockery in case these are smashed to provide a weapon.

Feelings

In the immediate situation they are likely to feel very frightened and over-whelmed by the power of their feelings. They may strongly regret pre-senting for help and the formal process of professional care that their behaviour has set in motion. Simple acknowledgement of their bravery in admitting their need for help and your affirmation that they have done the right thing can help to reduce their sense of vulnerability.

In the longer term, counselling and psychotherapy can be very helpful in allowing the individual to acknowledge, express and unravel compli-

	Early warning signs	Immediate response	Action
Table 2.6.1 Early warning signs and suggested responses	Frequent attendance for minor injury of an 'accidental' nature. *Be aware that many people who go on to attempt or commit suicide present at a health centre in the days or weeks prior to the final act.*	• Ask for very specific information about how the injury occurred. • Express your concern at the frequency and severity of the injury. • Question directly whether they did anything to cause injury. • Ask how they are feeling/whether anything significant is occurring in their life at present.	• Document clearly such that other staff are informed if they have future dealings. • Discuss with the GP/other practice staff. • Refer to the GP. • Carry out a formal risk assessment or arrange for this to be done.
	The patient attends in emotional crisis – very tearful, angry, frightened, distressed. Watchwords to look for are: 'Everyone would be better off without me', 'I won't be a problem to you for much longer', 'I wish I . . . weren't here/were dead', 'I'm beyond hope/help/', 'There is no hope/no way out', 'Nothing matters/everything is useless'.	• Make time to talk. • Ensure privacy. • Ask directly about suicidal thoughts, including whether they have thought about specific methods of self-harm. *There is no evidence that direct questioning about suicidal intent will put the idea in a person's mind and cause them to act on it; rather, it gives permission to discuss feelings openly, which is likely to come as a great relief.* • Ask about pessimistic feelings of hopelessness: 'How do you feel about the future?', 'Have you ever thought that life is not worth living?'. • Ask what stops them from attempting suicide.	• If necessary, delegate other work to colleagues, explaining your specific concern of suicide risk to the GP. • Identify and list known suicide risk factors in the patient's life. • Immediately refer to the GP. • Consider referral to a crisis management team if available. • May require psychiatric assessment and admission to hospital (compulsorily, under the Mental Health Act, if necessary). • Establish what support networks are in place – friends, family, distraction, activity, etc. • Discuss possible coping strategies.
	You notice injuries/scars on wrists, hands, arms of patients (particularly with teenagers, most commonly female), with the appearance of cigarette burns, superficial razor slashes.	• Ask directly how these occurred. • Probe gently: 'Did you do this to yourself?', 'How were you feeling when you did it?' *(many report feeling relief from tension, including sexual tension)*, 'How do you feel about it now?' *(many report feeling guilt, even disgust about their behaviour; for others it may be something of a 'badge' to wear)*, 'Does anyone know you do this?', 'Tell me about what is happening in your life at the moment'.	• Education regarding the consequences – unintentional serious harm, permanent scarring. • Establish what support network is available to them. • Identify any underlying psychological problems. • Identify any underlying social problems (consider possibility of physical/sexual abuse, a sexual identity crisis). • Consider referral for cognitive/behavioural therapy/counselling/psychotherapy.
	A patient you have been concerned about as at risk from self-harm or who has recently expressed suicidal ideas, presents in a seemingly elevated mood.	• Ask what has changed to bring about this difference. • Try to establish their plans for the next few days. • Express your concerns that their change of mood seems unrelated to any improvement in their life. *When depression is at its deepest, the sufferer cannot summon the energy or impetus to attempt suicide. One of the most risky times for self-harming behaviour is during treatment when mood lifts, but is not stable and established.*	• Be very wary if circumstances have not seemingly altered – the making of a firm decision to attempt suicide may bring about a lightening of mood because a 'way out' has been decided upon. • Carry out, repeat, or refer on for detailed risk-assessment.
	You suspect a patient of having taken an overdose.	• Immediately assess for vital signs – place in the recovery position if necessary. • Ascertain the medication taken: type, amount, how long ago and ascertain whether taken with alcohol.	• If unconscious/semi-conscious, call 999 for ambulance; even if the patient is well, seek medical attention. • Send empty medication bottles in with the patient. • Follow-up by primary health care services will be required to provide on-going support.

cated emotions that previously tied them in internal knots. To talk things
out in a non-judgmental climate of acceptance and respect can bring clar-
ity and allow a way forward to emerge. The relationship with the therapist can also provide support in itself. The process can be time-consuming
and expensive if outside the NHS, and progress may not always be steady
or even apparent – it is not a method that suits everyone – but the ' talking therapies', as they are sometimes referred to, are generally thought to
have a sound and established track record. Sometimes talking is not easy
and other methods of expressing feelings can be encouraged through art,
music and dance. Often a mixed programme of therapeutic activity can
provide the means for a comprehensive expression of feelings.

Thoughts
Cognitive therapy is often employed to help individuals explore the
thought processes and belief systems that lie behind and inform their behaviour. The theory is that this process of analysis will reveal illogical and
negative thinking patterns, allowing them to be challenged and replaced
with different ways of looking at life and the individual's place in it.

Behaviour
Cognitive behavioural therapy is very much linked to thoughts and tackles
these in conjunction with the consequent behaviour. It often involves carrying out practical tasks and gradually introduces new ways of responding to
stimuli that once set the sufferer off in a spiral of self-harming behaviour.

See Glossary for a more detailed explanation of the therapies
available.

◄ Key points

Treatment and management
- Maintain the safety of the suicidal individual – disarm them and
  supervise closely.
- They may require 999 to hospital.
- Obtain treatment for any physical injury already sustained.
- Refer on for psychological and psychiatric assessment and treatment.
- Provide immediate emotional support and reassurance.
- Devise a long-term plan for treating psychological distress.
- Consider counselling and cognitive behavioural therapy.
- Maintain a sensitive awareness to the stigma around suicide; help
  the patient/relative to deal with this.

The role of the primary health care nurse

The two points at which primary health care nurses are most likely to play
a key role are first, in identifying self-injurious behaviour and at a later stage,
perhaps after a patient is discharged from hospital after a suicide attempt. It
is also likely that they will be involved in supporting the relatives of people
who have attempted or committed suicide. Under these dramatic circumstances it is important to remember that the relative of the patient can quick-

ly become a potential patient themselves and will be vulnerable to suffering psychological and psychiatric problems as a result of their loss. They may go over and over why the person committed suicide, a question to which there will probably never be a conclusive answer: suicide is always an enigma.

Key points ➤

> **The role of the primary health care nurse**
> - To identify self-injurious behaviour.
> - To refer on for assessment and treatment.
> - To accept the patient back after hospital care, for on-going support.
> - To care for distressed relatives of the suicide victim, who in turn, are vulnerable to suicide.

Support groups, helplines and further information

Contact details and an explanation of the range of help and resources for each of the following organizations can be found in the 'A–Z of support groups' on pp. 134–154.

- Bristol Crisis Service for Women
- The Mental Health Foundation
- MIND
- Re-Solv
- Samaritans.

CASE STUDY 2.6.1

Mrs Barber, a middle-aged woman is referred by the GP to the practice nurse for a weekly blood pressure check because she has been prescribed an anti-depressant that can cause hypertension and for ' on-going support' because it is 3 months since her teenage daughter – an only child – committed suicide. (A suicide note confessed that she was a lesbian and could no longer cope with the double life she had been leading.)

How would you prepare for your first appointment with this patient?

- Speak with the GP for detailed information about treatment and management up to this point.
- Read up about both the grieving process and suicide.
- Read up about the specific anti-depressant medication.
- Find out about relevant voluntary organizations and local support networks, e.g. CRUSE.

Consider the various issues that this patient may well be dealing with.

- Issues of the daughter's sexuality, unnatural death by suicide, snuffing out of her daughter's potential and also her potential in relation to her daughter, unfulfilled desire to be a grandmother, out-living her daughter, becoming suddenly childless, the stigma of suicide.
- Dealing with acute emotions of grief, anger, bitterness, shame, guilt, sadness, loneliness and despair.

What will your plan of action be for providing on-going support?

- Start with the blood pressure and ensure that Mrs Barber understands all that is necessary about her medication.
- Establish what Mrs Barber feels she wants and needs of the appointment with you.
- Through initial conversation, build up a picture of her current support network: spouse, family, friends, groups, etc.

- Give information (if possible leaflets) about relevant voluntary organizations.
- Remember that Mrs Barber is also at risk of self-harm; consider using a risk of self-harm assessment.
- Keep in mind the need for referral on to counselling/psychology and/or psychiatric services.

CASE STUDY 2.6.2

Peter Mace is 18 and a first-year university student who has an appointment with the college nurse for removal of stitches from an arm wound. She notices a number of old scars on the young man's arm and asks how they occurred. He is vague and giggles rather fatuously, saying, 'Oh, you know, just accidents'. The nurse suspects that Peter is cutting himself.

How might the nurse follow up her suspicions?
- Build up a therapeutic relationship through general conversation and also try to uncover any areas of potential stress that might precipitate ' cutting'. Consider:
  - university course: has he made the right university/subject choice, pressure of work
  - university life: friends, activities, practical cooking/washing skills
  - life back home: parental support, pressure to achieve, homesickness
- Ask about stress and how he deals with it.
- Be direct about your suspicions and recognize that his scars are self-inflicted.

If Peter denies self-harm, how would you proceed?
- Document your suspicions.
- Speak to your line manager.
- Encourage him to make an appointment for a chat any time – emphasize that he doesn't need to have a physical problem in order to do this.
- Otherwise there is nothing to do – he is an adult and there are no rights to support talking to tutors or parents.

If Peter admits it, how would you advise him?
- Ask whether he wishes to stop and if so, refer on.
- Take some pertinent details for referral – how long he has been doing this, triggers to behaviour, thoughts when cutting, feelings afterwards.
- Offer him the opportunity to chat whenever he feels like cutting until such time as the referral is taken up.
- Provide any useful reading material and inform him about information on the Internet, which he might want to tap into using the university computers.

2.7   Eating disorders

Definition of eating disorders

Anorexia nervosa: – anorexia literally means 'loss of appetite'.

Bulimia nervosa: – bulimia literally means 'insatiable overeating'.

Although identified as separate eating disorders, many sufferers experience symptoms of both or move between conditions. Certainly both eating disorders revolve around a preoccupation with body weight, shape and image. However, it is misleading to dub an eating disorder as 'slimmer's disease', because the behaviour is usually a method of controlling and dealing with problems not directly connected to food.

Background

Anorexia nervosa has been recognized for over 100 years, whereas bulimia nervosa has only received mention in clinical reports and research since the 1970s.

Signs and symptoms

A distorted body image – a common and core sign of eating disorders – appears to have both a perceptual and an attitudinal component to it.

The perception is that they genuinely believe themselves to be far larger than they actually are.

One exercise commonly employed, where a sufferer is asked to draw an outline of their body shape, bears out this distortion, which can reach the level of a delusion.

The attitude is one of intense loathing of the look of certain body parts; for example they may believe that they have a huge and protruding stomach or gross cellulite on the thighs.

Distorted body image can be difficult for the outsider to relate to because it appears as such an obvious denial of the facts (see Figure 2.7.1 for details).

Causes

There are a number of different ideas about the causes of eating disorders. Certainly, the fact that it is a disorder particular to western society suggests that our obsession with body image – where 'tall and thin' are projected by the media as being the perfect body shape, which is highly valued – leads young people (who are more impressionable) to this particular behaviour in response to feeling stress and distress. This theory is strengthened by the fact that certain careers where thinness is valued even more highly, such as modelling and ballet, claim more than the average number of casualties to eating disorders.

Vulnerability factors

A number of common threads have been identified in case histories that suggests there are factors that make a person more vulnerable to developing an eating disorder.

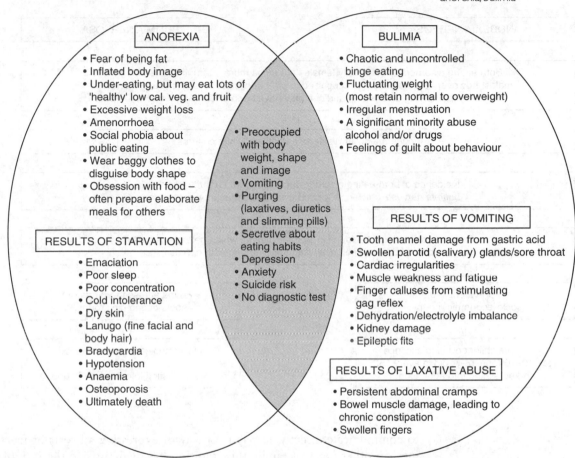

Figure 2.7.1

Signs and symptoms of anorexia/bulimia

ANOREXIA
- Fear of being fat
- Inflated body image
- Under-eating, but may eat lots of 'healthy' low cal. veg. and fruit
- Excessive weight loss
- Amenorrhoea
- Social phobia about public eating
- Wear baggy clothes to disguise body shape
- Obsession with food – often prepare elaborate meals for others

RESULTS OF STARVATION
- Emaciation
- Poor sleep
- Poor concentration
- Cold intolerance
- Dry skin
- Lanugo (fine facial and body hair)
- Bradycardia
- Hypotension
- Anaemia
- Osteoporosis
- Ultimately death

- Preoccupied with body weight, shape and image
- Vomiting
- Purging (laxatives, diuretics and slimming pills)
- Secretive about eating habits
- Depression
- Anxiety
- Suicide risk
- No diagnostic test

BULIMIA
- Chaotic and uncontrolled binge eating
- Fluctuating weight (most retain normal to overweight)
- Irregular menstruation
- A significant minority abuse alcohol and/or drugs
- Feelings of guilt about behaviour

RESULTS OF VOMITING
- Tooth enamel damage from gastric acid
- Swollen parotid (salivary) glands/sore throat
- Cardiac irregularities
- Muscle weakness and fatigue
- Finger calluses from stimulating gag reflex
- Dehydration/electrolyte imbalance
- Kidney damage
- Epileptic fits

RESULTS OF LAXATIVE ABUSE
- Persistent abdominal cramps
- Bowel muscle damage, leading to chronic constipation
- Swollen fingers

Personality

Personality traits of perfectionism and obsessional tendencies are commonly identified. Parents often report that as a child the sufferer was very compliant, obedient and well-behaved. This is often coupled with low self-esteem in adolescence, where the individual views him- or herself as lacking control and power.

Family

If this occurs within a family where there are high expectations for personal achievement, and perhaps successful siblings, the pressure is compounded. Eating meals together is a traditional part of family life and accepting and refusing food within the family can carry much deeper messages about accepting and refusing love: for an adolescent finding it hard

Figure 2.7.2

Incidence and distribution of
anorexia/bulimia

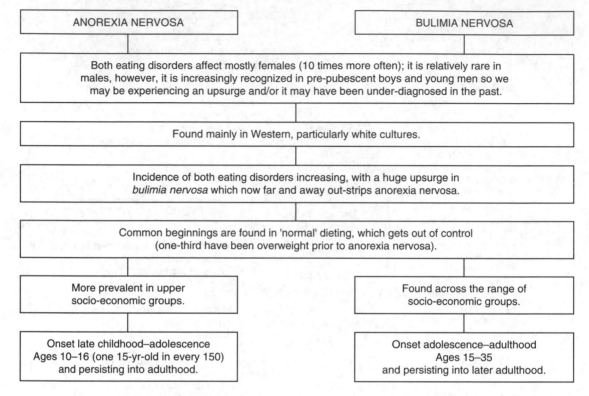

ANOREXIA NERVOSA	BULIMIA NERVOSA

Both eating disorders affect mostly females (10 times more often); it is relatively rare in males, however, it is increasingly recognized in pre-pubescent boys and young men so we may be experiencing an upsurge and/or it may have been under-diagnosed in the past.

Found mainly in Western, particularly white cultures.

Incidence of both eating disorders increasing, with a huge upsurge in *bulimia nervosa* which now far and away out-strips anorexia nervosa.

Common beginnings are found in 'normal' dieting, which gets out of control (one-third have been overweight prior to anorexia nervosa).

More prevalent in upper socio-economic groups.	Found across the range of socio-economic groups.
Onset late childhood–adolescence Ages 10–16 (one 15-yr-old in every 150) and persisting into adulthood.	Onset adolescence–adulthood Ages 15–35 and persisting into later adulthood.

to communicate directly, it may be a way of expressing all sorts of feelings. In other types of family this tradition has died away in the face of meals taken at different times and in separate rooms: this dissipation may be equally identified as a symptom of the loss of a cohesive family life. However, family dynamics are often identified as a cause of eating disorders – indeed, of many mental disorders – and this can become a most unhelpful exercise in apportioning blame and creating guilt.

It is significant that the incidence of eating disorders can often be found within the family history.

Physical traits
Eating disorders commonly begin with an overweight child dieting within normal limits: at some point this gets out of control. In anorexia one of the effects of starvation is that the process of puberty is delayed. This has led to theories of fear of sexual maturation being a key issue for the individual, where an under-developed body stalls the need to face up to the demands of growing up into adulthood and away from childhood.

Psychological traits

Upsetting life events are often identified as the trigger for the beginning of an eating disorder. These don't necessarily have to be negative in nature, but are likely to have been of sufficient significance to disturb the individual from their normal pattern of life.

In bulimia particularly, depression often starts a cycle of comfort eating: the comfort only lasts for as long as the food and soon after turns to disgust at the amount eaten, which leads to the need to purge, which results in guilt and depression, thus perpetuating the destructive cycle.

◄ *Key points*

Vulnerability factors
- *Personality traits:* perfectionist; obsessional; compliant, well behaved childhood; low self-esteem; experiences self as lacking power and control.
- *Family traits:* family history of eating disorders; high expectations for family members to achieve; loss of family tradition of cooking and eating together; food being used as currency to express or refuse love.
- *Physical traits:* difficulty accepting transition to sexual maturity – particularly in anorexia where puberty is delayed; initially overweight leading to 'normal' dieting behaviour, which spirals out of control.
- *Psychological traits:* depression – particularly in bulimia, where food becomes a comfort; response to upset, stress, pressure.

Perpetuating factors

Once an eating disorder is established there appear to be a number of perpetuating factors that maintain the behaviour and create a chronic, habitual pattern to the sufferer's way of life.

◄ *Key points*

Perpetuating factors
- Society/media pressure to be tall and thin and therefore valued.
- Peer pressure to conform to the notion of perfect body image.
- In anorexia, emotional elation at weight loss.
- In anorexia, a sense of empowerment at achieving weight loss.
- In anorexia, vigorous exercise creating a 'feel-good' endorphin release.
- In anorexia, starvation causing delayed gastric emptiness and rapid feeling of fullness after small intake of food.
- In bulimia, the relentless cycle of binge–comfort–guilt–purge, which is so difficult to break.

Management

Presenting for treatment

Very few sufferers of anorexia or bulimia present for treatment; they are more likely to be referred by worried family, friends, teachers or the school nurse. Some may present directly, but with a related problem, such as gastric symptoms or menstrual abnormalities; they are unlikely to admit upfront – least of all to themselves – to suffering from an eating disorder. There is no diagnostic test for either disorder, but detailed history taking usually reveals a clearer clinical picture (see SCOFF in Section 3, p. 120). However, bulimia is more easily disguised because body weight is usually within acceptable proportions and the sufferer is likely to remain very secretive about extreme eating and purging behaviour. It is advisable that a physical assessment be carried out at the initial stage, including taking blood to check for electrolyte imbalance and anaemia, and calculating of body mass index (BMI).

In-patient or out-patient care

Hospital management of anorexia has undergone vast changes in the last 10 years, mostly due to a shift in focus from equating weight gain alone to health gain. In the past it was common for a strict behavioural regime to be imposed on the sufferer whereby they maintained a certain dietary intake and remained on bedrest under constant nursing supervision until agreed weight targets were reached. Failure to comply resulted in loss of privileges, such as visits from friends. Admission to hospital for bulimia has been less common, but now both disorders are often treated on a psychiatric out-patient basis. Referral to specialist eating disorder units is indicated for those with particularly concerning and/or entrenched disorders.

Ironically sufferers of eating disorders frequently feel a lack of control and power in their lives, but are often experienced by others as being manipulative and controlling.

Recognition and acceptance

The initial starting place for treatment lies with the sufferer accepting that they have a problem for which they require help. Keeping a food diary where they report on eating habits over the course of a week can help to show the individual themselves that they have a problem. This can provide particularly stark proof for someone with bulimia, who is faced with the chaos of their normal eating habits. One model for viewing an eating disorder is to see it as representing an individual's (maladaptive) attempt to cope with life. Successful treatment therefore lies in finding a more productive, less dangerous method of coping. With this model it is clear that to merely restore normal weight by a process of imposing strict regimes on the sufferer risks a speedy return to a disordered eating pattern once the regime is lifted. Many hang on doggedly to their illness fearing the loss of control and any direct confrontation of underlying problems. Co-operation with treatment may be an on-going process requiring patience, understanding and continuing support from family, friends and health care professionals.

Management
- A move away from previous emphasis, where the equation was seen as: achieving normal weight = back to normal health.
- The individual's acceptance of need for help is a key first step.
- Identify and tackle individual mechanisms behind the eating disorder.
- Monitor eating habits and triggers to disordered eating.
- Graduate steps towards 'normal' eating.
- Use of behavioural, cognitive and psychotherapeutic methods of treatment.
- Use of family therapy and group therapy.
- Complementary therapies are often of benefit.
- Self-help groups, books and leaflets are also often beneficial.
- Refer to dietician for education about normal diet.

Individualized care programme
There is increasingly greater emphasis on understanding the individual mechanisms behind the behaviour and tackling them on an individual basis. This is likely to involve a mixture of different approaches: cognitive (identifying and tackling the thought processes that inform the person's behaviour), behavioural (ignoring or penalizing negative behaviour and rewarding positive behaviour) and psychotherapy (supportive counselling). These therapies may include a mixture of individual and group sessions. Family therapy is also commonly employed (the whole nuclear family attend and participate to identify group dynamics and patterns of behaviour that may be causing and perpetuating problems, and to explore new ways of being together).

Complementary therapies
Therapies involving talking and sharing feelings may be a difficult and slow process for many. Complementary therapies which largely rely on non-verbal techniques, such as art and music therapy, as well as aromatherapy and massage have been found to make a useful contribution to the overall treatment programme. Self-help groups are also of enormous benefit to some, especially in easing the sense of social isolation. There are a number of self-help books and pamphlets available and autobiographical works of people who suffer from an eating disorder, which may provide useful information and encouragement to sufferer and supporter alike.

Normalizing eating patterns
Alongside these therapies attention will be paid to normalizing eating and reaching a healthier weight, as well as tackling purging behaviour. Re-education about food values and achieving a balanced diet is a component of this. Graduating the steps towards 'normal' eating is recommended. Identifying the triggers to disordered eating can also be an enlightening

exercise. Some individuals respond well to contracts for behaviour, while others find these rigid and automatically wish to kick against them.

Medication

Medication, such as appetite stimulants and tranquillizers are not commonly used, but anti-depressant therapy for underlying depression may well be indicated.

Eating disorders and the role of the primary health care nurse

The primary health care nurse may be the first port of call for a relative or friend anxious about someone they suspect is suffering from an eating disorder, or a problem may be uncovered when a sufferer attends for a related, or indeed, unrelated problem. Awareness of early warning signs is an advantage, helping to nip a problem in the bud before it becomes a full-blown eating disorder. The primary health care nurse may also be assigned a role following in-patient or out-patient care for someone with an eating disorder. Disordered eating can become a habitual way of dealing with stress and similar patterns of behaviour may re-emerge when stress is encountered in the future. The primary health care nurse may be in the perfect position to recognize this and begin early intervention.

A thorough and ordered initial assessment by the nurse will prove invaluable to the GP and specialists. This should identify the following:

- a list of observed signs and symptoms
- current eating/purging habits
- current underlying problems and life stresses
- relevant family history
- present physical status: weight/height (BMI), vital signs (bradycardia/hypotension?)
- urinalysis (keytones/kidney function?).

Early referral on, usually via the GP, will help to speed up the sufferer's access to appropriate treatment. Continuing care will include monitoring eating behaviours and subsequent physical health of individual sufferers. In addition, the primary health care nurse may well be called upon to provide psychological support for the individual sufferer and their family, including talking over specific worries that are contributing to the problems. Part of this process includes referral to self-help groups and providing educational literature and information.

Increasingly primary health care nurses are being called upon to give general input at local schools and youth clubs in providing education about such issues as eating disorders and this certainly provides a most valuable service in promoting healthy eating habits and preventing serious health problems.

The role of the primary health care nurse
- To pick up early warning signs of eating disorders.
- Initial assessment and referral to a specialist.
- On-going monitoring of patients with eating disorders.
- Psychological support for sufferer and family.
- Provision of information about resources available, including literature.
- Education and health promotion in local schools and youth clubs.

Support groups, helplines and information

Contact details and an explanation of the range of help and resources for each of the following organizations can be found in the 'A–Z of support groups' on pp. 134–154.

- Bristol Crisis Service for Women
- Eating Disorders Association
- First Steps to Freedom
- The Mental Health Foundation
- MIND
- Overeaters Anonymous.

CASE STUDY 2.7.1

You are becoming increasingly concerned about a district nurse colleague who you suspect of developing bulimia nervosa. There have been a steadily mounting number of signs: something of a weight/diet obsession, reading dieting magazines, always talking about joining a slimming club, declining to join the staff meal, chocolate wrappers galore in the car, missing lunch breaks, and so on. However, the most recent indication – the stock of laxatives diminishing far quicker than expected after this colleague has been on duty for the weekend – is the most serious, for the individual's health and in terms of her professional behaviour.

What is your next step?
- Consider the issue of the professional misconduct of taking laxatives alongside the personal crisis of a colleague. Speak to the colleague directly. Find a private location and enough time to really tackle her.

How would you persuade her to recognise her problem and seek appropriate help?
- Guard *against* using the issue of stealing laxatives to blackmail her into owning up to her eating disorder.
- Face her with the signs you and others have noticed. Point out how serious things have become and that the disorder now has control of her.
- Be sympathetic about the distress she must be feeling – emphasize that your prime concern is helping her to get the help she clearly needs.

CASE STUDY 2.7.2

A family planning nurse is consulted by a young couple who have been trying for a baby for over a year without success. They attend together for the initial meeting where the husband takes control of the conversation. He stresses how health conscious they both are and seems to feel betrayed by the fact they have not achieved a pregnancy. He clearly feels the problem lies with his wife whose menstrual cycle, they both agree, has always been 'up the creek'. The nurse notes that the woman is very slim and particularly notices her thin and dry looking hair and skin. She is conscious that she allows her husband to speak for her. When she takes a history the woman claims nothing of significance in past medical health, but her husband interjects to say 'except as a teenager when you were in hospital for anorexia'. This statement has quite an impact on the woman who laughs in a brittle fashion and retorts defensively that this was ages ago.

What are the indications that the woman may still have an eating disorder?
- The woman may have reverted to a previous eating disorder behaviour in the face of stress – the 'grown-up' and expected step of having a baby following marriage is perhaps more the husband's desire than her own.
- She may have fertility problems related to previous anorexia.
- She shows clear physical indications that she may verge on being anorexic – low body weight, thin hair, dry skin.
- Her husband behaves in a controlling way during the interview. She is equally controlling in her dismissal of previous anorexia as having been significant in her medical history, which is tantamount to a denial of any current problem.

2.8 DEMENTIA

Definition of dementia

Dementia is a complex illness which combines features of chronic neurological disease, mental illness, physical frailty, communication problems and a high level of difficulty for carers.

Making Sense of Dementia, Annual Review
Alzheimer's Disease Society, 1996/97, London ADS

Dementia is not a single disease, but rather a syndrome; a generic term describing global cognitive (intellectual) impairment, which is progressive and irreversible, while consciousness remains clear and unaffected (until the terminal stage). Gradual forgetfulness, disorientation and confusion describes the typical dementia picture.

Reaching a diagnosis

There are differential diagnoses to consider before a diagnosis of dementia is reached and there are a number of different types of dementia. However, most follow a similar course and it is often only after post-mortem that an unequivocal diagnosis is reached.

When dementia is suspected a detailed assessment is required – ideally at the earliest possible time. The degree of impairment may be concealed by the individual patient's ability to maintain a good social facade and therefore use of a specialist psychometric tool for assessment – such as the Mini Mental State Examination (see Section 3.1, p. 125) – is highly recommended.

Acute confusional state	• Toxicity: alcohol/drugs/prescribed medicines (often 'poly-pharmacy' in the case of the elderly) • Infection: respiratory/urinary tract • Endocrine disorder: diabetes/thyroid problems • Metabolic disorder • Dehydration and electrolyte imbalance • Malnutrition: vitamin deficiency • Epilepsy • Cardiovascular disease/crisis: poor perfusion/anoxia • Raised intercranial pressure: haematoma/haemorrhage/tumour • Severe emotional trauma • Brain metastases secondary to a primary carcinoma.	**Table 2.8.1** Differential diagnoses of dementia
Depression	Can impair cognitive functioning.	
Normal ageing	Some memory impairment is normal with old age – not to be confused with the more serious diagnosis of dementia.	

Key points ➤

What is dementia?
- Dementia is a generic term that covers a number of signs and symptoms.
- The key feature is progressive and irreversible intellectual impairment, in clear consciousness.
- The major differential diagnoses are acute confusional state, depression and the effects of normal ageing.
- There are a number of different types of dementia, which relate to the particular cause of the disease.
- Detailed assessment using a specific psychometric tool is highly recommended.

Causes of dementia

The different types of dementia relate directly to the particular causes of dementia. The two most common categories are Alzheimer's disease (senile dementia) and multi-infarct dementia. The former is caused by

Table 2.8.2

Causes of dementia

Cause of dementia	Type of dementia	Description
Degenerative	Alzheimer's disease	Gradual, progressive global deterioration.
	Lewy body disease	Psychotic features of hallucinations and delusions; includes many Parkinsonian features; rapid deterioration.
	Parkinson's disease	Late feature of disease for approx. 30% of sufferers.
	Multiple sclerosis	Late feature of the disease.
	Pick's disease	Rare, early onset – before 65; prominent mood changes: lack of concern, shallow emotions and disinhibited behaviour; intellect less affected.
	Frontal dementia	Very similar to Pick's disease.
	Huntington's chorea	Late feature of disease, but still usually before 65.
Vascular	Multi-infarct dementia	Sudden onset with 'step-wise' deterioration.
	Binswanger's disease	Past history of hypertension; slow onset, with specific neurological signs.
Mechanical	Subdural haematoma	Sudden onset of dementia – reversible if treated early.
	Normal pressure hydrocephalus	Early onset – reversible if treated early.
Infections	Syphilis	Late feature of the disease.
	Prion-dementias: Creutzfeldt-Jakob's disease	Causes 'spongiform encephalopathy', which results in dementia.
	HIV and AIDS	Late feature of the disease.
Metabolic and endocrine	B_{12} or thiamine deficiency	Causes dementia with a key feature of disturbance of balance and vision resulting in difficulty walking.
	Hypothyroidism	Particularly associated with depression and lethargy.
Toxic	Korsakoff's syndrome from chronic alcoholism	Confabulation – compensating for memory loss by creating plausible explanations – is a key feature.
	Heavy metal poisoning Liver/kidney disease	

degeneration and death of brain cells leading to brain shrinkage, and the latter is caused by mini strokes, as emboli disrupt the blood supply, causing softening of the brain tissue by infarcts. Alzheimer's disease, which accounts for more than half of all dementias, has no known cause, although there is some evidence of a genetic predisposition. The underlying cause of multi-infarct dementia is cerebrovascular disease.

◄ *Key points*

What causes dementia?
- The various causes of dementia are degenerative, vascular, infection, toxicity and metabolic and endocrine disorders.
- Dementia occurs at an end-stage of many chronic illnesses, such as multiple sclerosis and Parkinson's disease.
- The two most common types of dementia are Alzheimer's disease and multi-infarct dementia.
- Alzheimer's disease is caused by degeneration of brain cells and brain shrinkage.
- Multi-infarct dementia is caused by cerebrovascular disease.

Incidence and distribution

Dementia becomes more common with increasing age. It is less common before the age of 65, when it is sometimes referred to as pre-senile dementia, and where the progression of the disease is often swifter and more aggressive.

Onset:	
	Before 65 = rare
	65–74 = 1%
	75–84 = 10%
	85+ = 25%

Women are more likely to suffer from Alzheimer's disease and men more commonly suffer from multi-infarct dementia. Specific figures differ according to sources, but the following bar-chart gives a proportional representation of the incidence of the major causes of dementia in the UK.

Prognosis

Some early symptoms of dementia can be treated effectively. For example, drugs are being developed to help preserve cognitive functioning, but in time the effects are irreversible. In Alzheimer's disease the survival rate is, on average, about 7 years, where the deterioration is gradually downhill at a steady pace towards an end-stage where full nursing care is required. Multi-infarct

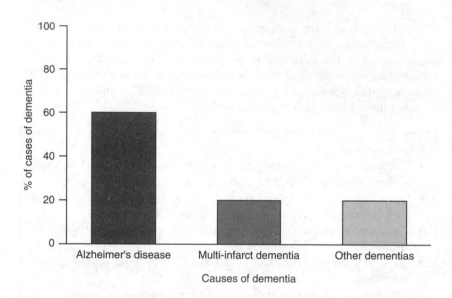

Figure 2.8.1

Bar chart showing causes of
dementia

dementia holds a slightly worse prognosis of 5 years, where deterioration
occurs in downward steps as cerebrovascular infarcts occur at intervals, and
where there is always the possibility of sudden death from a stroke.

Key points ➤

Who is affected by dementia?
- Dementia becomes more common with increasing age.
- Dementia is uncommon before the age of 65, when it is referred
  to as pre-senile dementia.
- Women are more likely to suffer from Alzheimer's disease.
- Men are more likely to suffer from multi-infarct dementia.
- With Alzheimer's disease the survival rate is about 7 years.
- With multi-infarct dementia the survival rate is about 5 years.
- With Alzheimer's disease deterioration is gradual and irreversible.
- With multi-infarct dementia step-wise deterioration occurs as
  infarcts occur.
- Intervention to prevent infarcts can be successful, but there is always
  the possibility of sudden death from a stroke.

Signs, symptoms and features of dementia

The sufferer themselves may be the first to realize that they have a problem – often when memory problems begin to interfere with everyday life
– and they may even suspect dementia to be the cause. However, many
channel their energy into hiding and denying their problems, fearing that
they are losing their ability to function in the world and maintain their
grasp on life. Consequently it is often a relative who presents to the GP
with their concerns. The signs, symptoms and features of dementia concern every area of life in an increasingly devastating fashion.

Early stages	Later stages
Cognitive	
• Short-term (recent) memory deficits	• Long-term memory is also impaired
• Difficulty learning and retaining new information	• Language problems: receptive and expressive dysphasia – forgets words/uses wrong words
• Impaired spatial and visuoperceptual ability	• Some suffer from delusions and hallucinations (often visual and auditory)
• Impaired spatial and visuoperceptual ability	
• Concrete thinking evident – not able to reason	
Emotional	
• Shallow mood	• Extreme mood swings
• Emotionally labile – irritable/excitable	• Hostile
• Suspicious	• Aggressive
• Lack of responsiveness/empathy for others	• Flat affect (mood)
• Depression and anxiety	
Behavioural	
• Difficulty in handling complex tasks	• Perseverance – prolong or repeat a response after original stimulus ceases
• Accident-prone	• Restless
• Disorientation for time and place	• Disorientation for time, place and person
• Disturbed sleep	• Wandering – often nocturnal
• Social withdrawal	• Turn night into day
• Self-neglect	
• Agitation and restlessness	
• Disinhibition and odd behaviour	
• Attention demands – clingy behaviour	
Physical	
• As a result of disorientation, patient becomes incontinent, unable to see to physical needs satisfactorily	• Emergence of primitive reflexes
	• Immobility
	• Rigidity – muscle contractures
	• Tremor
	• Epileptiform seizures
	• Fluctuating consciousness
	• Total dependence on others for physical needs

Table 2.8.3

The signs, symptoms and features of dementia

◄ **Key points**

What are the effects of dementia?
- The sufferer may be the first to suspect that they have dementia, but go to great lengths to conceal it.
- It is often a relative who presents to the GP with their concerns.
- The symptoms affect every area of functioning:
  - physical
  - emotional
  - behavioural
  - cognitive.
- Symptoms become progressively severe, to an 'end-stage' where full nursing care is required.

Management of dementia

The management of dementia is complex because the disease impacts on the life of each patient in a particular and individual way and needs will change at varying rates as the disease makes its inevitable progress towards a need for total care. An additional element to management is that the patient needs to plan for a time when they will no longer be in charge of their faculties. The maintenance of dignity and individuality – when the patient is no longer able to maintain this for themselves – are central to all treatment and management interventions.

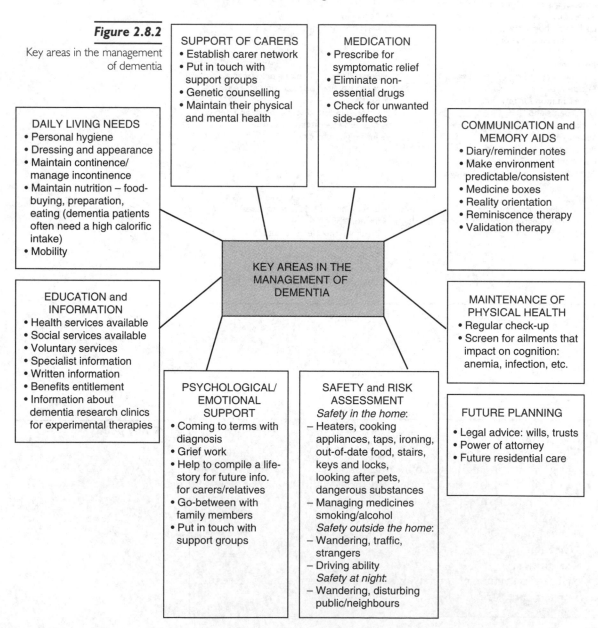

Figure 2.8.2

Key areas in the management of dementia

SUPPORT OF CARERS
• Establish carer network
• Put in touch with support groups
• Genetic counselling
• Maintain their physical and mental health

MEDICATION
• Prescribe for symptomatic relief
• Eliminate non-essential drugs
• Check for unwanted side-effects

DAILY LIVING NEEDS
• Personal hygiene
• Dressing and appearance
• Maintain continence/ manage incontinence
• Maintain nutrition – food-buying, preparation, eating (dementia patients often need a high calorific intake)
• Mobility

COMMUNICATION and MEMORY AIDS
• Diary/reminder notes
• Make environment predictable/consistent
• Medicine boxes
• Reality orientation
• Reminiscence therapy
• Validation therapy

KEY AREAS IN THE MANAGEMENT OF DEMENTIA

EDUCATION and INFORMATION
• Health services available
• Social services available
• Voluntary services
• Specialist information
• Written information
• Benefits entitlement
• Information about dementia research clinics for experimental therapies

MAINTENANCE OF PHYSICAL HEALTH
• Regular check-up
• Screen for ailments that impact on cognition: anemia, infection, etc.

PSYCHOLOGICAL/ EMOTIONAL SUPPORT
• Coming to terms with diagnosis
• Grief work
• Help to compile a life-story for future info. for carers/relatives
• Go-between with family members
• Put in touch with support groups

SAFETY and RISK ASSESSMENT
Safety in the home:
– Heaters, cooking appliances, taps, ironing, out-of-date food, stairs, keys and locks, looking after pets, dangerous substances
– Managing medicines smoking/alcohol
Safety outside the home:
– Wandering, traffic, strangers
– Driving ability
Safety at night:
– Wandering, disturbing public/neighbours

FUTURE PLANNING
• Legal advice: wills, trusts
• Power of attorney
• Future residential care

Specialist therapies for use with dementia

Reality orientation
This is a technique used to help people who are confused and disorientated to make sense of their environment and to give it meaning. It uses cues and activities to provide reminders about who the person is, why they are there and about their immediate and wider surroundings.

Validation therapy
This was born out of a realization that not everyone is open to reality orientation all the time and that there is meaning behind whatever someone says or does, however confused or muddled the words or behaviour seem on the surface. It does not collude with the person's confusion, but rather, accepts that this is *their* reality and is therefore valid and has meaning. It is particularly helpful in facilitating communication of feelings and enabling carers to support the person emotionally.

Reminiscence
This is valued as a therapy for patients with dementia for a number of reasons. Above all it is relaxing and gives great pleasure: long-term memories often remain intact and require no struggle to recall. Remembering who they were provides sufferers with much needed validation at a time when they feel they are losing their sense of self. Equally, the carer benefits by hearing about a past life that speaks of the individual behind 'the patient with problems'. Household objects, old photographs, clothes, songs and music all help to spark memories and oil the process of reminiscence. Memorabilia are often available for hire from local museums and local libraries are a good source for archive material.

Examples of different approaches to responding to confused thoughts
A patient persistently asks what time the train is due.

Reality orientation: reorientates the patient to the actual environment and reassures them that there is no need to worry anymore about catching trains.

Validation therapy: explores the patient's confused idea by asking where she thinks she has to go to by train . . . work? . . . to visit someone? Is she worried about missing someone or something? Is she remembering commuting to work everyday? Is she wishing to escape from something or is she excitedly anticipating a journey somewhere?

Reminiscence: asks about where she used to travel by train, allowing the reminiscence to flow, with one memory sparking the next. Particularly fond or keen memories can be a focus, along with memorabilia – old photos, pictures, artefacts – which add to the experience.

Each approach is valid and at different times one response might be more appropriate than another.

Key points ➤

> **What can be done?**
> • Management of dementia must cover:
>   – daily living needs
>   – safety and risk assessment
>   – medication
>   – communication and memory aids
>   – physical health
>   – education and information about dementia
>   – future planning needs
>   – psychological/emotional support
>   – support of carers.
> • Future care must be planned for when the patient is no longer in charge of their faculties.
> • Maintenance of dignity and individuality throughout is key.
> • Reality orientation, validation therapy and reminiscence are useful therapies for patients with dementia.

Medication and dementia

Medication can have both beneficial and adverse effects on the course of dementia.

Therapeutic effects

• There are increasingly more medications coming on the market that appear to slow the cognitive deterioration of certain patients with certain types of dementia. All patients should be carefully screened to ensure that they fit the prescribing criteria.
• Disorders causing or contributing to the dementia should be corrected with medication; for example, anti-coagulants for those with multi-infarct dementia.
• Medication should be used to improve the general physical state; for example, by treating anaemia.
• Unwanted secondary symptoms of dementia such as depression, anxiety, insomnia and agitation can be controlled with medication.

Adverse effects

• Overuse of medications and unwanted interactions between medications may cause or exacerbate problems significantly.
• Sedatives can exacerbate confusion as well as contributing to the risk of falling.
• Over-sedation can deplete any remaining cognitive function.
• Medication can decrease renal function and cause electrolyte imbalance, further compromising physical health and complicating the dementia picture.
• Over-concentration and emphasis on medication distracts attention away from equally important and relevant non-medical aspects of dementia, e.g. social problems.

Medication and dementia
Therapeutic effects of medication:
- Improve cognitive function for some patients.
- Correct disorders that cause or contribute to dementia.
- Improve general physical health.
- Provide symptomatic relief.

Adverse effects of medication:
- Poly-pharmacy confuses the clinical picture.
- Risk of over-sedation.
- Side-effects cause dehydration, electrolyte imbalance and renal impairment.
- Over-medicalization and emphasis on the physical side of the condition.

Caring for the carers

Most people with dementia live at home (80%) and half of these live with a carer, most of whom are relatives. For those living alone, most have carers (often relatives again) coming in on a regular basis. It must not be assumed that those remaining in their own homes only suffer mild impairment from dementia. Many are severely impaired and totally dependent on their carers, who often have little or no support and are at significant risk of suffering physical and/or mental illness as a consequence.

An awareness of the difficult areas and issues for each particular carer is useful – it helps to target support accurately. Common problems include day and night-time wandering, confused and repetitive conversation, a need for regular respite and practical support and advice.

Day and night-time wandering
The aim is to maintain the balance between keeping the person safe and allowing them as much freedom as possible (see 'Case study 2.8.1', p. 102).

Confused and repetitive conversation
This may cause frustration and embarrassment for the patient and be equally trying for the carer. Increasingly the patient will lose insight about this problem and therefore feel less upset by it; however, the irritation and upset provoked in their carer may well still impact on them.

Regular respite
To be really useful and restorative, respite needs to be regular and planned in advance such that it can be looked forward to, rather than arranged in an emergency when the carer is on their knees and at their wits end. Respite might be a few hours off a week, or a day away here and there, or a week – or more – on holiday. It might be someone coming in to help or the patient being taken out. Local health and social services, as well as charitable and voluntary organizations dealing with dementia, can give more information about what is on offer in your locality.

Tips for effective communication
- Face the person, maintain eye contact, talk slowly and clearly.
- Use visual cues and gestures.
- Use short sentences and familiar words.
- Talk where background noise is at a minimum – switch off TV and radio.
- Explain something *before* you begin to do it. For example, don't start helping the person into a coat while saying, 'Let's put your coat on so we can go out'.
- Try not to be offended if they forget your name – remind them who you are in a natural way.
- Don't draw attention to their failing memory. The emphasis of 'Don't you remember?' doesn't help to jog a memory that isn't there.
- When conversation is repetitive, try to steer it elsewhere by distracting them onto another topic.
- Try to identify the feelings and emotions behind confused talk – and connect with that, rather than with the words.
- If the person is trying to tell you something and you don't understand, ask them questions they can answer with a simple 'Yes' or 'No' or one-word reply.
- It is understandable to feel irritation, even anger, but showing this will increase agitation and compound the problem. Leave the room for a while, look out of the window, take a deep breath. Remind yourself that this is as much a symptom of the disease as breathlessness is to an asthmatic – mum/dad/whoever really cannot help it.

At the same time, remind yourself that you are doing a great job in coping.

Practical and emotional support and advice
Caring for a dependent person can be physically, emotionally, mentally, and financially exhausting. Mere acknowledgement of the burden of caring is sometimes of help in itself. There is also the family of the carer to consider and the way in which it impacts on them.

Key points ➤

> **Caring for the carers**
> - Many people with severe dementia remain at home looked after by carers – often relatives – with little or no support.
> - Carers themselves are at risk of suffering from physical and mental ill health.
> - Difficult areas include:
>   – day and night-time wandering
>   – confused and repetitive conversation
>   – need for regular respite
>   – practical support and advice.
> - The impact of caring ripples out to the carer's family.

The role of the primary health care nurse

The role of the primary healthcare nurse depends upon the stage at which the patient presents: you may be the first to suspect the early stages of dementia through other contact with the patient, in which case the initial role will be in putting the assessment process in motion. You may come in at an end-stage, co-ordinating care, or involved in a particular aspect of care. You may, indeed, have more input with supporting relatives who are carers than dealing with the patients themselves. The patient is vulnerable to a number of forms of abuse – physical, sexual, emotional and financial – and one sensitive role you may need to handle is keeping a vigilant eye for any signs of abuse.

◄ Key points

The role of the primary health care nurse
- To pick up early signs of dementia.
- Screening for dementia.
- Assessment to confirm the diagnosis of dementia.
- To take part in a specific aspect of care.
- To co-ordinate care within a nursing and/or mixed disciplinary team.
- To support relatives and carers.
- To maintain vigilant watch for any signs of abuse of the patient – physical, sexual, emotional or financial.

Support groups, helplines and further information

Contact details and an explanation of the range of help and resources for each of the following organizations can be found in the 'A–Z of support groups' on pp. 134–154.

- Age Concern England
- Alzheimer's Disease Society
- Carers National Association
- The Mental Health Foundation
- MIND
- Parkinson's Disease Society of the United Kingdom
- The Princess Royal Trust for Carers.

CASE STUDY 2.8.1

Mr and Mrs Arnold, an elderly couple, have been referred to the health visitor. Mr Arnold has Alzheimer's disease and is cared for at home by his wife. Lately he has taken to leaving the house and wandering, by day or by night, and although he has always found his way back safely he is clearly vulnerable and Mrs Arnold is anxious about the situation.

As the health visitor, how might you advise and assist in this case?

Things to try to ascertain (from both Mr and Mrs Arnold):
The purpose of the wandering:

- Is it to get somewhere or to see someone?
- Is it part of a generalized restlessness?
- Is walking a previously enjoyed hobby?

The pattern of the wandering:

- Does it occur at the same time?
- Does it occur as the result of a particular trigger?
- Is the same route usually taken?
- What is their mood before and after?
- Do they say anything before or after, however muddled it may seem?

This information may throw light on what lies behind the wandering behaviour. For example, it might be triggered initially by Mr Arnold needing the toilet and setting off to find one, or he might be bored and need to be occupied with a distracting activity.

Working with the behaviour:
- Try to build planned walks into the day, perhaps accompanied by friends, relatives or other carers – try local rambling group for volunteers.
- Give the walk added purpose by going to the shops or the library or to visit someone.
- If night-wandering increases advise trying to tire Mr Arnold during the day to induce better sleep.

Some practical measures to take:
- A bolt can be placed at the bottom of the outside door where it is less obvious for him to look for one. Locking him in might seem overzealous, but could just be used at night when he is more vulnerable.
- A 'shop bell' could be fitted to alert Mrs Arnold when he is leaving.
- He could wear an identity bracelet in case he gets lost and cannot give his own personal details.
- Sew reflective material onto his overcoat and keep this by the door so he is likely to put it on before going out. Put useful items in the pockets, such as gloves, a small torch, sweets so that he can keep energy levels up when he does wander.
- Inform local police of the on-going situation.
- Inform local shop-keepers, etc. to keep a look-out.
- Consider medication, especially if Mr Arnold is distressed when he is wandering in a confused fashion.
- Consider Mrs Arnold's need for respite care for her husband.

CASE STUDY 2.8.2

A district nurse makes a monthly visit to Mr Penn to monitor his diabetes. He remains well, but is not his usual cheerful self and when Mrs Penn leaves the room he says, 'she's losing it in the head'. Mrs Penn has a diagnosis of dementia but her usual mild muddle has recently been interspersed with episodes of suspicion when she accuses her husband of tampering with her pills. Yesterday she wouldn't eat her supper, saying he had poisoned it.

What are the various elements that need to be dealt with in this situation?

Mrs Penn:

- Refer back to the community psychiatric nurse – who she currently sees once a month – for urgent reassessment.
- Check what medication she is taking and consider its effects – contact the GP if necessary.
- Consider her nutritional needs if meals are being missed.

Mr Penn:

- Deal with his immediate distress: he is hurt by the accusations and concerned about his wife's behaviour.
- Explain that paranoia can be a feature of dementia and to try to view it as a symptom of the illness.
- Increase visits to monitor his diabetes more closely until the situation improves.
- Refer Mrs Penn for respite care – perhaps a day centre – where food is provided and medication can be given.

2.9   Life's stresses and adjustment

Our lives are punctuated by events that unsettle the equilibrium and require adjustment to allow normal function to be resumed. These events may be for good or ill and the adjustment required may be a slight tweak or a complete re-think and a major change. The events may be related to the various milestones of our life (also termed developmental crisis), such as marriage, having children, reaching retirement and facing the inevitability of death, or there may be unexpected occurrences (also termed 'accidental crises'), such as serious illness, moving house and job loss. All of these can certainly cause stress, and stress can provide one of the triggers for causing or exacerbating a mental illness.

Key points ➤

What is stress?
- Life milestones include getting a job, marriage, having children, retirement.
- Life-events include moving house, severe illness, bereavement, redundancy.
- Life-milestones and life-events can represent good or ill.
- Both require adjustment and can cause stress.
- Stress can cause and/or exacerbate mental illness.

For health professionals, awareness of where a patient stands in terms of life-milestones, as well as any specific life events that have occurred is useful: it provides a background against which to assess the 'problem' with which a patient presents.

The milestones of life

The milestones identified in Figure 2.9.1 represent a fairly conventional Western way of life and, therefore, cultural and chronological differences should be allowed for when considering this subject. It is possible that the age range of your patients embraces every age from childhood to old age. Within a particular specialist area of nursing it might be useful to plot more detailed milestones for your particular patient group.

Potential life-events

Life-events are often construed in terms of positive or negative when, in fact, there may be a down-side to a seemingly joyous event – the demands of a new-born baby, the media pressures brought by a cash windfall – and equally there may be hidden advantages in a difficult circumstance – a relationship strengthened by facing adversity together, doors of opportunity opened when redundancy leads to a search for a new job. Many life-events and milestones overlap each other and one event might compound the problems already experienced by another, or indeed cause another event to occur in a domino effect. For example, infertility and the pain of child-

Figure 2.9.1

The milestones of life

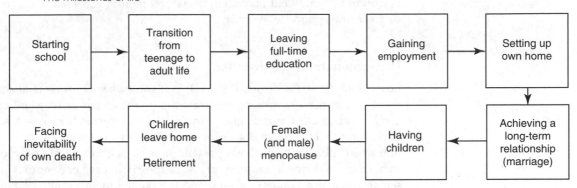

Life-event	Positive	Negative
Money concerns	• Cash windfall: inheritance, prize-money, maturity of financial investment, insurance pay-out, pay rise	• Cash flow problems: rent or mortgage, arrears, overdraft, loans, credit-card overload, unpaid bills
Relationships	• New relationship: in love • Deciding to live together/get married • Starting a family • Having children • Forging new friendships	• Disharmony • Divorce • Alimony wrangles • Child custody battles and access visits • Sibling rivalry • Step-children/parental difficulties
Education	• Changing school • Leaving school • Starting a course • Starting university • Passing exams	• Failing exams • Bullying • Negative peer group pressure
Health	• Taking on a healthy lifestyle: reaching and maintaining optimum weight/fitness • Overcoming serious illness • Living successfully with chronic illness/disability • Adjusting to effects of surgery, prosthesis, etc.	To self or those close to you: • Serious sudden illness: myocardial infarction/stroke, etc. • Serious or chronic illness diagnosed: cancer, Parkinson's, diabetes, etc. • Undergoing surgery • Fertility problems • Unwanted pregnancy • Accident • Post-traumatic stress • Death and bereavement
Employment	• Getting a job • Embarking on a new career • Being promoted • Starting a business • Welcome retirement or redundancy	• Job loss • Redundancy • Overlooked for promotion • Bullying • Job dissatisfaction • Work overload
Location	• Moving house • Moving area	• Social isolation • Geographical isolation • Overcrowding

Table 2.9.1

Life-events and their possible effects

lessness might lead to financial crisis as large amounts of money are spent to have IVF treatment. The significance of a life-event will also differ from person to person: what may seem trivial to one may represent something of great importance to another.

Post-traumatic stress disorder

Post-traumatic stress disorder (PTSD) is a somewhat controversial diagnosis in that there is disagreement among professionals as to whether it can be said to exist as a distinct condition. However, it is included here in recognition of the fact that primary health care nurses are on the front line when it comes to patients presenting with health and life problems that occur following a traumatic crisis. Be aware that the patient may present to you many months or even years after the traumatic event took place.

Key points ➤

> **Causes of traumatic stress**
> - Road traffic (or similar) accidents
> - Sudden or violent bereavement
> - Sexual attack or abuse
> - Physical assault
> - Survived or witnessed a disaster, such as train crash, earthquake, flood, etc.
> - Wartime experience
> - Torture or hostage experience

Symptoms of post-traumatic stress disorder

Post-traumatic stress has come to be viewed as a distinct diagnosis because key features of a disorder can be identified among those who have suffered a recent traumatic event or who have suffered chronic problems since a past traumatic event. When a patient is referred to you with PTSD or one presents whom you suspect of suffering from PTSD, you will probably find it useful to apply knowledge about the 'stress adjustment process'.

The key features of post-traumatic stress disorder

- Distressing recollections of the event – where it is remembered
- Flashbacks to the event – where it is renewed
- Insomnia and nightmares
- Anxiety and irritability
- Frequent crying
- Hypervigilance – being over-careful and watchful
- Startle easily – jumpy and tense
- Sense of doom
- Poor concentration
- Blank out memories of the event
- Blunted feelings towards loved ones
- Avoidance behaviour related to the event

- Loss of interest in activities that were previously enjoyed
- Children may regress and lose previously achieved milestones and skills.

Stages of adjustment

The study of bereavement has given some insights into the *process* involved in coming to terms with death; a process of gradual adjustment. 'Process' is a key word to bear in mind because it reminds us that although progress might be slow – to the point of two steps forward and one back – and at times might halt altogether, things will probably move forward – however slowly – on the journey of recovery. Reassurance that recovery will come might give comfort and hope to all those involved in the process. We may attempt to speed people up out of their suffering, often because we cannot bear to witness their distress, or it resonates with psychological distress of our own that we do not wish to face. However, this is usually counter-productive. When people learn that they are suffering from a chronic or terminal illness they embark upon a similar adjustment process to that of the bereaved: they mourn their loss of function and the loss of the future they had planned. They may search for a cure and go to great expense and outlandish lengths in an attempt to forestall the inevitable; this represents a sticking point in the adjustment process, in which, as primary care nurses, you may become embroiled. The process of adjustment can be usefully applied to many situations other than death that also involve loss, such as the breakdown of a relationship or leaving 'home' and moving to a new area.

The normal stages of the grieving process

- Shock and disbelief
- Acute emotional responses:
  - *Anger*   Crying, shouting, being engulfed by waves of
  - *Guilt*   intense grief, feeling anxious and tense, showing signs
  - *Pining*   and symptoms of depression
  - *Sadness*
  - *Hopelessness*
  - *Despair.*
- Acute behavioural responses:
  - searching for the 'lost' person/situation
  - ruminating – going over the past
  - preoccupied thoughts
  - physical, emotional and social withdrawal.
- Gradual acceptance, resolution and recovery.

NB: Set-backs may occur on the occasion of anniversaries.

Problems with adjustment

There are sometimes sticking points in the process of adjustment and it is most likely that these will bring the patient to your attention.

Psychosomatic symptoms

It may be clear to the patient what the problem is when they present for your help, but for the most part it is less clear-cut. The patient's

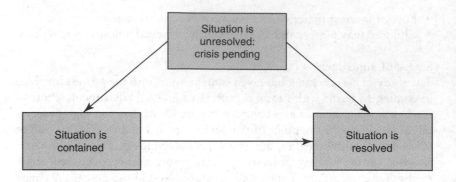

difficulty in adjusting might come in another guise, often where psychological pain has been transposed into physical symptoms, known as somatization or conversion. Common psychosomatic symptoms include sleep disturbances, chest pain, palpitations, headaches and gastric and bowel disturbances. To dismiss psychosomatic symptoms as unreal is a serious error: they are usually very real, but relief from them is unlikely to be obtained until the root (psychological) problem is dealt with. Uncovering the psychological pain beneath the physical symptoms becomes the first step towards health.

'Learned helplessness'
'Learned helplessness' may also hinder the adjustment journey, where the patient has come to rely so heavily on others that they fail to recognize or utilize their own inner resources in the process. The power of learned helplessness can be seductive when it over-emphasizes the importance of the 'carer' who may come to be viewed – equally by the 'carer' herself – as being indispensable to the patient. Empowering the patient in their own recovery is always the goal.

A defence mechanism is a protective device used to shield us from feeling emotional pain. One example of a defence mechanism might be a sense of humour, which allows us to laugh and joke in the face of disappointment. While this might be useful, positive and adaptive at times, it can also work against us by preventing us from experiencing the full depth of an emotion; it might also prevent us from sharing at an emotionally deep level with other people. Some believe that individuals who are 'over-defended' fail to deal effectively with their emotional pain, causing it to surface in other ways, such as in physical or mental illness. Decompensation describes the inability to apply protective and adaptive defence mechanisms as a coping strategy when faced with a stressful situation. As a result, non-coping is exacerbated.

Assisting patients to proceed in the adjustment process

Crisis management
This may be the first step in the adjustment process – it is the alarm informing that all is not well. It may have reached this head because of a mal-

> **Problems with adjustment**
> - An unresolved situation may herald a future crisis.
> - Psychosomatic symptoms mask the underlying problem.
> - 'Learned helplessness' disempowers and prevents resolution of the situation.
> - Over-defensiveness and decompensation are the two maladaptive extremes of defence mechanisms.

adaptive way of coping with the stress of a life milestone or life-event, for example making a suicide attempt. Patients present because they do not have the required resources to meet the crisis: you may have the necessary resources to offer yourself, or within the team you work in, or you can refer on to an appropriate source.

De-briefing
Allow the patient to go over and over the situation and events in order to fully ventilate their feelings – this may need to be taken on by a trained counsellor. Where you have expertise, give honest straightforward explanations, sometimes using diagrams or charts to provide clear information, literally in black and white. The patient may wish to take this away to refer to again (and again) and to show to friends and family who support them.

Developing coping strategies
When a patient is overwhelmed by a crisis they feel helpless: a step-by-step approach will help them to claw back control and will hopefully be an empowering experience. Break the situation into small adjustment tasks that are achievable, in order to gain an increasing sense of mastery. Mal-

Short-term	Long-term
• Crying	• Seeking help
• Angry and aggressive outbursts	• Seeking information
• Sleeping more	• Being gentle with/looking after self
• Withdrawing and avoiding people	• Re-evaluating situation
• Using (abusing) alcohol, cigarettes, drugs	• Making plans – carrying these through
• Over/under-eating	• Learning new skills
• Overspending – shopping sprees	• Confronting problems – tackling people
• Complaining	• Setting short-term targets and long-term goals
• Humour – laughing things off	• Long-term goals
• Avoiding/denying a problem	• Making changes to self and situation
• Rationalizing the problem to remove or under-emphasize its impact	• Becoming open to alternative ideas
• Projecting difficulties onto someone else to make it *their* problem	• Diverting attention from the problem
• Displacing emotions that properly lie with the problem onto another focus	

Table 2.9.2

Coping strategies

adaptive coping strategies may have become entrenched and need to be replaced with positive ones. Short-term coping strategies are not necessarily maladaptive, but used repeatedly in the long-term prove inadequate for shifting the individual to a more positive position.

Promoting a problem-solving approach

Help the patient to create an action plan, brainstorm potential resources to assist them, set realistic goals towards change, develop a system of self-reward and reinforcement and give guidance and support throughout this process. Encourage the patient to evaluate progress, but guard against viewing unmet goals in terms of failure, and instead encourage them to try a different tactic.

Dealing with stigma and labelling

The nature of the crisis, or, indeed, the maladaptive coping strategy used to try to deal with the crisis may have led to the patient being stigmatized within their family, peer group or the wider community. This can be a stumbling block on the road to recovery, particularly when the stigma persists long after the crisis subsides. Boosting the patient's sense of self and belief in themselves such that they can rise above ridicule or censorship is key. Opportunities may arise to educate family and friends of the patient and even the wider community about the negative impact of stigma and how it often arises from ignorance and fear.

Support

Reassurance and encouragement throughout the process of adjustment is vital. As well as providing one source for this yourself, try to mobilize others: assist the patient in thinking of people in their 'circle' who might provide support. Refer on for counselling support and support from voluntary agencies where appropriate.

Promotion of mental health

The primary health care nurse is in an excellent position to promote mental health, such that the crisis which might have precipitated mental illness becomes instead a turning point in the patient's life. You can help in the development of a healthy life-style and increase awareness of unhealthy coping strategies, which might lead to future mental health problems; for example, using alcohol in a habitual fashion to feel at ease in social situations. You can teach problem solving techniques which empower the patient to take back control in a step-by-step approach to solving difficulties. You can play an important role in educating people about the facts rather than the fears about mental illness and aim to reduce its negative impact when it does occur.

Assisting in the adjustment process
- Crisis management.
- De-briefing.
- Developing coping strategies.
- Promoting a problem-solving approach.
- Dealing with stigma and labelling.
- Support.
- Promotion of mental health.

Support groups, helplines and information

Contact details and an explanation of the range of help and resources for each of the following organizations can be found in the 'A–Z of support groups' on pp. 134–154.

Carers
- The Princess Royal Trust for Carers

Child-related
- Action for ME
- AD/HD Support Groups UK
- Anti-bullying Campaign
- Hyperactive Children's Support Group (HACSG)
- Young Minds

Menstruation
- PMS Help
- Premenstrual Society (PREMSOC).

CASE STUDY 2.9.1

Eva Sharp attends the health visitor-run group for women who wish to lose weight. She has recently been investigated for a breast lump – found to be malignant – and is to have a mastectomy imminently. In the group she is very matter-of-fact and jokes about it saying it's one quick way to lose weight. She remarks that she's lost her ticket into the group now as weight-loss is not advisable at the moment. There is lots of hilarity and banter among the women who remark on her amazing attitude.

As the health visitor, how would you describe Eva's response to her situation?

- Joking and 'laughing it off' is potentially a double-edged sword of a defence; it holds value as a coping mechanism, but could equally block her from grieving for her loss, such that she never really accepts her self-image without her breast. The words she uses – 'ticket into the group' – suggests regret at no longer being a group member.

How would you respond to her and to the group?

- Find an opportunity to speak with her alone. See if there are chinks in the bravado and whether she would value talking more, either with you or with a specialist counsellor.
- Find out whether she has unanswered questions about her condition and provide answers and reading material.
- Consider and discuss her remaining as a group member for the mutual support it provides and put her in touch with any local mastectomy support groups.
- Provide a channel of communication between the group and the individual while she undergoes treatment.
- Suggest a cohesive activity for the group such as a sponsored slim or exercise class for a specific breast cancer charity.
- Seize the health promotion opportunity and provide educational material about the importance of breast self-examination and answer any queries that arise from the group.

CASE STUDY 2.9.2

Thomas Fletcher is referred by the GP to the practice nurse for 'general support' after investigation of frequent headaches uncovers no physical cause. The patient has recently lost his job after 25 years and the GP is sure this is connected.

As the practice nurse, what questions do you think it would be pertinent to ask?

- What does he think is happening? What are his ideas about cause?
- What does he think will help? What would he like of her input?
- What is his network of personal support – friends, family?
- Build up a picture of his personal history through conversation.

What do you think is going on with Mr Fletcher?

- He is somatizing feelings about loss of job and financial worries in the form of headaches.
- He is failing to break with work and move on.
- He is too stuck in his predicament to look for work or to improve his situation.

What could you offer to support him?

- The headaches are his focus: and he genuinely feels pain even if the cause isn't physical so, tackle the headaches: diary of symptoms, time of day, food eaten, sleep, other triggers, etc.
- Consider diet, posture, exercise, relaxation techniques.
- Try to find some ways of shifting his focus from the headaches.
- Broach the subject of redundancy and what this means to him.
- Seek out local resources and schemes for unemployed.
- Assess for signs of depression and indications that he may be seeking escape through alcohol, for example.
- Consider referral on to psychology/psychiatry services.
- Discuss complementary therapies that might be beneficial (aromatherapy, massage, etc.).

RESOURCES

3.1 PSYCHIATRIC ASSESSMENT

You cannot measure anxiety in the same way you can measure your hat size.

Testing People, J. Beech and L. Harding (p. 2)

Background

The concept of assessment is no different for mental health problems than for physical ones. The primary health care nurse is familiar with making 'new patient assessments' and assessing and reviewing the on-going condition and treatment of patients with, for instance, diabetes, hypertension or asthma, and the underlying concept is exactly the same for a patient with, for instance, depression or schizophrenia. It is sound nursing practice to carry out regular systematic reviews with patients receiving regular treatment from you, such as a patient with schizophrenia to whom you administer a regular anti-psychotic depot injection (see pp. 121 for an example of a suitable questionnaire for these patients).

If you suspect that a patient may be developing or suffering from mental health problems, it is useful to carry out a formal assessment, which highlights significant signs and symptoms and may well contribute to the process of making a formal diagnosis.

If an incident – such as an aggressive outburst – occurs, an 'on-the-spot' assessment can be carried out, which helps to clarify the situation and form a considered response, rather than just rushing in (see Table 3.1.2, pp. 117).

◄ Key points

> **What is assessment?**
> - The concept of psychiatric assessment is no different from any physical assessment.
> - It is sound nursing practice to carry out regular reviews of your care of patients with mental health problems.
> - A 'Present Mental State' assessment is a useful tool for identifying mental health problems.
> - Instant assessment – when an unexpected incident occurs – provides clarity, overview and helps to form an appropriate response.

The aims of psychiatric assessment and review

To review the care of a patient is to think about the person and what you are doing with them in a formal way: to draw back from the immediate interventions and treatment, allowing for an overview, which will identify any change for good or ill and include aims for future outcomes. For those who find such structures rigid and prefer to work more intuitively, it should be noted that the use of a system does not preclude intuition, but rather provides a structure to back up those nursing decisions which, if analysed, are largely based on intuition and experience. Professional accountability is held in high regard and a systematic approach to assessment and review certainly helps to support and maintain this. However, there is a potential tension between, on the one hand, becoming bogged down with the paperwork involved and, on the other hand, using it to target care accurately while also saving time and resources.

Key points ➤

> **The aims of assessment and review**
> - To provide a comprehensive overview of the situation.
> - To provide a baseline against which to monitor for change – for better or worse.
> - To contribute towards establishing a diagnosis.
> - To plan care, interventions and referrals in a systematic way.
> - To evaluate nursing care plans and interventions.
> - To predict future care needs.
> - To identify specific risk factors.
> - To provide documented back-up for nursing care decisions.
> - To aid professional accountability.
> - To provide information for colleagues and other involved professionals.
> - To provide clear and concise information for family/carers.

Methods of assessment and review

Assessment can be undertaken using a variety of methods: the authors recommend carrying out a regular, structured interview using predetermined questions in a set format. Use of a questionnaire does not preclude more general, free-flowing conversation, which will compliment a formal, structured approach by eliciting different kinds of information while helping to build a therapeutic relationship. Throughout any interview observation skills, to pick up non-verbal cues, should be applied to further inform an understanding of the situation. Use of psychometric tools – there are many, most related to a specific mental disorder or related aspect of care – provides a score that relates to a scale measuring the severity of the symptoms or situation. This is particularly useful when repeated at regular intervals, for identifying changes over time with a patient. It is advised that initial training, guidance and supervision are sought before using a particular psychometric test. It should always be remembered that these are just tools, as are all questionnaires: they assist in the process but are not the 'be all and end all' of care!

> **Methods of assessment and review**
> - Structured interview, using pre-determined questions in a set format.
> - Unstructured interview, gleaning pertinent information from the general conversation.
> - Psychometric tool, such as Beck's inventory for depression.
> - Observation of non-verbal information.

Advantages	Disadvantages
Written questions ensure that no area is overlooked.	They are not tailored to individuals and may fail to elicit person-specific information. The nurse may feel limited and constrained by the questions.
Repetition of the same questions, asked in the same way, reveals changes over time and highlights improvement or deterioration.	There may be over-reliance on the questionnaire to the exclusion of picking up other cues or making other interventions, i.e. failure to remember that it is just a tool to assist and inform care.
Some patients prefer the formality: it may be perceived as less intrusive and personal for patients than the general talk of an unstructured interview.	It may be perceived as impersonal and cold for patients.
The nurse is somewhat shielded from the awkwardness of obtaining information of an intimate nature by using a questionnaire to 'ask the questions for her'.	
It assists with the recording and presentation of information.	There is potential to accumulate piles of paperwork, which is then not looked at or applied.
Information can be stored on computer and used for audit purposes (profiling GP practice, for example) or research.	There is a need to maintain strict confidentiality and to protect access to information.

Table 3.1.1

Advantages and disadvantages of a structured questionnaire

The skills required for assessment and review

Nurses are involved in assessment and review in almost every aspect of their work.

Gaining the co-operation of the patient is the first step and if they do not wish to answer the questions that is their prerogative; they cannot be made to participate. However, while patient co-operation is vital, written consent is not required unless the information elicited is to be put forward as part of a research study. During assessment and review the following skills are operating:

The outcome of assessment and review

It is important that the information gathered from assessments and reviews does not become just so much paperwork, which fails to be applied in a

Figure 3.1.1

Skills required for assessment and review

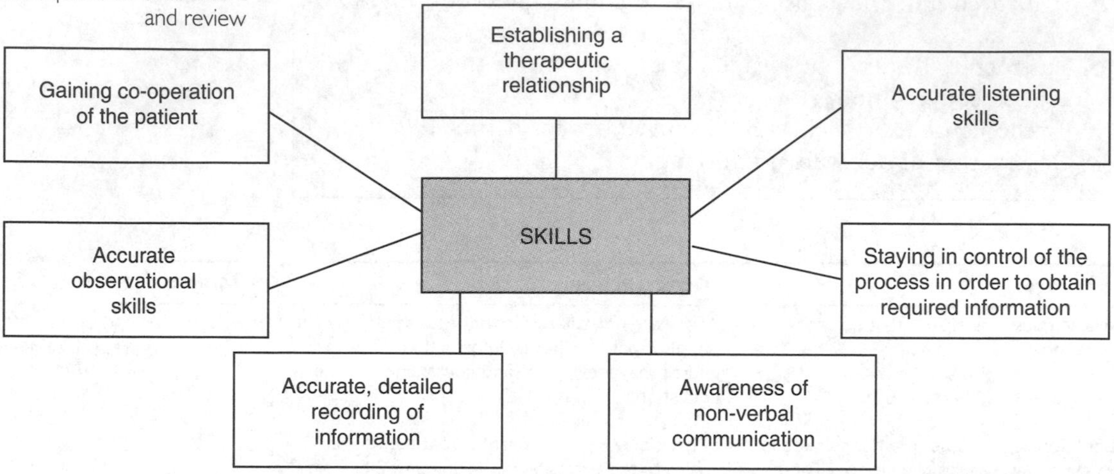

practical way to the care of the patient. In addition to guiding on a day-to-day basis, care assessments and reviews can usefully be shared with other involved professionals. These may indicate the need to refer certain aspects of care on to others, or indeed to stop an aspect of care that emerges as being irrelevant. Many nurses find discharging patients from their care very difficult and may continue to keep certain individuals on the caseload to avoid the finality of discharge: recorded structured reviews can be useful in underlining the need for closure of an individual's care, for the nurse and patient alike. Around all these decisions an awareness of confidentiality is vital: let the patient know who will see the questionnaires and reassure them about confidentiality issues.

Key points ➤

> **The outcome of assessment and review**
> • Knowing when and with whom to share information.
> • Appropriate referral on to other professions and agencies.
> • Identifying the appropriate time for discharging a patient.
> • Awareness of issues of confidentiality.

Assessment and management of aggression

Aggressive and violent incidents are relatively rare but it is advisable to be aware of techniques to assess and manage such situations appropriately. If you work alone and visit patients in their own home the following precautions are advisable:

• Attend 'control and restraint' courses and keep updated.
• Carry a mobile phone.
• Inform 'base' where you are and when to expect you back.
• Make initial joint visits with a colleague to assess a patient with whom you are unfamiliar.

Assess degree of danger to patient and others	• Punches or objects being thrown, person making physical contact, loud threats of violence:
	  – *Serious*: phone 999 for police back-up and evacuate area;
	  – *Containable*: invite person to discuss away from the public area and stimulation of others, phones etc. *However,*
	• Have back-up within reach if situation escalates.
		Table 3.1.2
		
		Assessment and management of aggression

Establish cause/provocation	• Under influence of drugs, alcohol, glue, etc. • Acute stress from life event. • Reacting to psychotic features of a mental illness: hallucinations, delusions. • Intense frustration, especially where they feel powerless. • Confusion and disorientation. • Over-stimulation heightening arousal levels. • Habitual way of reacting – often aggressive.	
De-escalation of situation	• One person to speak with the patient – differing viewpoints from different quarters will not be helpful. • Diminish the anger – encourage *talk, sit down*, allow plenty of *personal space* between you, make *eye contact*, watch *tone and volume level of voice* (avoid ridicule, sarcasm, threats, being patronizing), *show concern* (calm may be impossible to achieve) *remain polite, but not distant* (be real and convey that you are a person with feelings too, not just part of an impersonal system). • Acknowledge the strength of feelings felt – the upset behind the anger. You don't have to agree with the behaviour, but can still affirm the patient's experience. • Clarify the problem – ask 'How?', 'What?', 'When?'. But avoid the more provocative question of 'Why?'. Use active listening skills such as repeating back what the patient says, 'reflecting' and 'paraphrasing'. • Solve the problem – working with the patient, which may require compromise, flexibility and concessions. • Inform them about how to make an official complaint and help them if this is desired.	
Creating a more conducive environment	• Physical environment: guard against overcrowding in communal areas, provide distractions and 'comforts'. • Manner of personnel – training in dealing with the public. • Personal demeanour – non-threatening body language, facial expression, manner and tone of speech.	
De-briefing	• Talk with those involved, upset, and witnesses. • Staff group discussion about incident. • Acknowledge feelings: fears may well be appropriate, inadequacies may indicate need for training/support. • Reconsider protocols to deal with such incidents. • Consider safety measures required to be taken. • Incidents should be documented.	

- In an unfamiliar situation, position yourself such that a quick exit is possible.
- If a patient is aggressive towards you, even verbally, *leave immediately* and summon help if necessary.
- Document any incident and report to your senior management.

Tools for assessment

The series of questionnaires and tools that follow may prove useful in your work: you may photocopy them as they are, or use them to adapt to your own requirements.

Risk of suicide assessment

If you suspect a patient is suicidal the following 'indicator questions' can be asked to confirm your fears. Refer on to relevant professionals – regardless of questionnaire outcome – if you remain concerned (the patient might be denying their true state of mind).

If the patient has suicidal ideas but with no intention to act, a useful extra question is to ask 'What stops you?'. It might be family, responsibility for children, religious belief or any number of things. The information gives an insight into how they tick and is useful to focus on for encouraging and supporting them as they struggle with their depression.

Figure 3.1.2

Indicator questions for risk of suicide

INDICATOR QUESTIONS

1. Do you feel that life is no longer worth living?
   (Motivation)

   SUICIDAL IDEAS
   in the absence of an
   INTENTION TO ACT
   = LOW RISK

2. Have you felt like acting on this?
   (Intentions)

   SUICIDAL IDEAS
   and
   INTENTION TO ACT
   = MODERATE RISK

3. Have you made any plans to carry this through?
   (Specific method planned and ability to do it)

   SUICIDAL IDEAS
   and
   INTENTION TO ACT
   and
   SPECIFIC PLANS
   = SEVERE RISK

4. Have you ever tried to harm or kill yourself before?
   (Past history)

   'YES' TO Q. 4
   INCREASES
   OVERALL RISK

Drink diary

This drink diary is particularly useful in identifying triggers to the undesired behaviour and confronts the person with their own behaviour, literally in black and white. It can be adapted for eating disorders and other addictions.

SENSIBLE DRINKING GUIDELINES

1 unit alcohol = 1/2 pint beer, lager, cider
(extra strength may measure twice this)
small glass of wine
single pub measure of spirits

Women: 2–3 units daily or less
Men: 3–4 units daily or less

	WOMEN	MEN	RISK
Units per week	14	21	Little risk to health
	14–35	21–50	Increasing risk to health
	35+	50+	Risk of dependence and very risky to health

Note: If elderly, pregnant, on incompatible medication or have known health problems, unit intake should be lowered.

Figure 3.1.3

Sensible drinking guidelines

Day	Time	Where	Who with Type of drink	No. of drinks		How you felt before drinking	How you felt after drinking
					= __ units		
					= __ units		
					= __ units		
					= __ units		
					= __ units		

Table 3.1.3

Example of a drink diary (Source: Health Education Authority and Alcohol Concern)

119

CAGE – a screening tool for suspected alcohol addiction

These questions are designed to confirm suspicion that an alcohol addiction might exist. It is recommended that this is included as part of a new patient check or lifestyle review, as well as where alcohol addiction is suspected.

It is for use by non-specialists – particularly in primary care. It should be noted that this tool is less reliable at identifying those who are at risk from much lower alcohol consumption levels – such as pregnant women.

Table 3.1.4

CAGE questionnaire (Source: Ewing, J.A., 1984, Detecting alcoholism: the CAGE questionnaire. *JAMA*, 252, 1905–7)

	YES	NO
Have you ever felt you ought to *cut down* on your drinking?		
Have people *annoyed* you by criticizing your drinking?		
Have you ever felt bad or *guilty* about your drinking?		
Have you ever had a drink first thing in the morning ('*Eye-opener*') to steady your nerves or get rid of a hangover?		

Score 1 point for every 'YES'. A score of >2 indicates the need for a more thorough assessment. A score of > 3–4 strongly suggests alcohol abuse.

SCOFF – a screening tool for suspected eating disorders

These questions are designed to raise suspicion that an eating disorder might exist.

It is for use by non-specialists – particularly in primary care.

Table 3.1.5

SCOFF questionnaire (Source: Morgan, J., Reid, F. and Lacey, J.H., 1999, The SCOFF questionnaire; assessment of a new screening tool for eating disorders. *British Medical Journal*, 319, 1467–68)

	YES	NO
Do you make yourself *Sick* because you feel uncomfortably full?		
Do you worry you have lost *Control* over how much you eat?		
Have you recently lost more than *One* stone in a 3-month period?		
Do you believe yourself to be *Fat* when others say you are too thin?		
Would you say that *Food* dominates your life?		

Score 1 point for every 'YES'. A score of >2 indicates the need for more rigorous, specialist clinical assessment.

Review of patient on maintenance depot anti-psychotic medication

This questionnaire should be carried out every 8–12 weeks.

Patient name: Date:	YES	NO	PROBLEM/ COMMENT	ACTION TAKEN
Tick relevant boxes				
Physical symptoms (provides a basic screening in case you are the only health worker who is regularly seeing the patient): How have you been feeling physically? Have you had more trouble sleeping than usual? Have you had any pains anywhere lately? Have you developed any lumps anywhere? Have you had unusual bleeding from anywhere lately? Has your appetite or eating pattern changed?				
Anxiety: Have you felt more anxious, frightened or tense lately?				
Depression: How cheerful have you been? Have you felt more depressed: very sad/maybe tearful?				
Delusions: Have you been worried that people are talking about you, plotting against you, or trying to harm you? Is there anything special about you that would make anyone want to do that?				
Hallucinations: Have you been hearing noises or voices, or seen strange things, when no one was about and there was nothing else to explain it?				
Thought content: Have you any problems with your thinking? Have you any problems with loss of concentration/jumbled or racing thoughts?				
Daily occupation: Do you have somewhere to go out to on most days?				
Apathy: Have you managed to get up and out most days?				
Medication: Have you suffered any side-effects from your depot since we last met?				
Social support: Is there anyone who you can really count on for help in a crisis? Is there anyone – or maybe a pet – who really counts on you?				
Appointments: Have you seen the GP since we last met? Have you seen a CPN/psychiatrist in OP dept/any other mental health care worker?				
Bizarre behaviour: Postures, grimaces, flippant remarks, loss of social restraint				

Table 3.1.6

Review of patient on maintenance depot anti-psychotic medication questionnaire (Source: Burns, T., Kendrick, A. and Millar, E., 1995). This questionnaire should be carried out every 8–12 weeks.

Table 3.1.6

(Continued) Review of patient on maintenance depot anti-psychotic medication questionnaire

Patient name: Date: Tick relevant boxes	YES	NO	PROBLEM/ COMMENT	ACTION TAKEN
Slowness, underactivity: Sits abnormally still, moves very slowly, says very little, poor eye contact				
Anxiety: Tense, nervous gestures, sweating profusely *Depressed mood*: Tearful, sad or blank expression, flat affect (mood) *Hostility*: Irritable, verbally or physically aggressive *Self-neglect*: Clothes, hygiene, nutritional status *Incoherence of speech*: It is difficult to make sense of what the patient says; they may have 'made up' words, or verbalized a rush of ideas that you couldn't follow				
Medication side-effects: (if you wish record as: mild [1], moderate [2], severe [3]): Parkinsonian – tremor, stiffness, rigidity, stiff and expressionless face, dribbling/drooling Akathisia – distressing restlessness (shuffling feet and legs), and they may comment that they can't keep still Tardive dyskinesia – facial squirming and grimacing, thrusting of trunk, odd jerking arm and leg movements OTHER: please record below:				
Brief additional comments: Please record below if *anything significant*, either *positive or negative* in nature, has happened in the patient's life since their last appointment, e.g. may have got married/divorced/suffered a bereavement/lost or gained a job/moved house/begun a new relationship/financial loss or gain, etc.				

Figure 3.1.3

POST-NATAL DEPRESSION QUESTIONNAIRE

Mother's name: .... Telephone number: ....

Address: ....

Today's date: .... Baby's age (weeks): ....

Health visitor: .... Mother's age: ....

GP: ....

As you have recently had a baby, we would like to know how you are feeling now. Please UNDERLINE the answer which comes closest to how you have felt IN THE PAST WEEK, not just how you feel today.

Here is an example, already completed.

I have felt happy:

> *Yes, all of the time*
> <u>*Yes, most of the time*</u>
> *No, not very often*
> *No, not at all*

This would mean 'I have felt happy most of the time' during the past week.

In the past week:

1. I have been able to laugh and see the funny side of things:

    As much as I always could.
    Not quite so much now.
    Definitely not so much now.
    Not at all.

2. I have looked forward with enjoyment to things:

    As much as I ever did.
    Rather less than I used to.
    Definitely less than I used to.
    Hardly at all.

3. I have blamed myself unnecessarily when things went wrong:

    No, never.
    Not very often.
    Yes, some of the time.
    Yes, most of the time.

4. I have been anxious or worried for no good reason:

    No, not at all.
    Hardly ever.
    Yes, sometimes.
    Yes, very often.

5. I have felt scared or panicky for no very good reason:

    Yes, quite a lot.
    Yes, sometimes.
    No, not much.
    No, not at all.

6. Things have been getting on top or me:

    No, I have been coping as well as ever.
    No, most of the time I have coped quite well.
    Yes, sometimes I haven't been coping as well as usual.
    Yes, most of the time I haven't been able to cope at all.

7. I have been so unhappy that I have had difficulty sleeping:

    Yes, most of the time.
    Yes, sometimes.
    Not very often.
    No, not at all.

8. I have felt sad or miserable:

    Yes, most or the time.
    Yes, quite often.
    Not very often.
    No, not at all.

9. I have been so unhappy that I have been crying:

    Yes, most of the time.
    Yes, quite often.
    Only occasionally.
    No, not at all.

10. The thought of harming myself has occurred to me:

    Yes, quite often.
    Sometimes.
    Hardly ever.
    Never.

Figure 3.1.4

Post-natal depression scale: scoring system (Source: Cox, J., Holden, J. and Sagotsky, R. (1987). Detection of post-natal depression. *British Journal of Psychiatry*, **150,** 782–786). This questionnaire is designed for the mother to complete during an appointment – stay with her to answer any queries

POST-NATAL DEPRESSION QUESTIONNAIRE SCORING SYSTEM

A score of 12 or more indicates there may well be post-natal depression and the patient should be referred for more detailed psychiatric assessment. Remember, these are guidelines only and not diagnostic instruments.

In the past week:

1. I have been able to laugh and see the funny side of things:

   0 As much as I always could.
   1 Not quite so much now.
   2 Definitely not so much now.
   3 Not at all.

2. I have looked forward with enjoyment to things:

   0 As much as I ever did.
   1 Rather less than I used to.
   2 Definitely less than I used to.
   3 Hardly at all.

3. I have blamed myself unnecessarily when things went wrong:

   3 No, never.
   2 Not very often.
   1 Yes, some of the time.
   0 Yes, most of the time.

4. I have been anxious or worried for no good reason:

   0 No, not at all.
   1 Hardly ever.
   2 Yes, sometimes.
   3 Yes, very often.

5. I have felt scared or panicky for no very good reason:

   3 Yes, quite a lot.
   2 Yes, sometimes.
   1 No, not much.
   0 No, not at all.

6. Things have been getting on top or me:

   3 No, I have been coping as well as ever.
   2 No, most of the time I have coped quite well.
   1 Yes, sometimes I haven't been coping as well as usual.
   0 Yes, most of the time I haven't been able to cope at all.

7. I have been so unhappy that I have had difficulty sleeping:

   3 Yes, most of the time.
   2 Yes, sometimes.
   1 Not very often.
   0 No, not at all.

8. I have felt sad or miserable:

   3 Yes, most or the time.
   2 Yes, quite often.
   1 Not very often.
   0 No, not at all.

9. I have been so unhappy that I have been crying:

   3 Yes, most of the time.
   2 Yes, quite often.
   1 Only occasionally.
   0 No, not at all.

10. The thought of harming myself has occurred to me:

    3 Yes, quite often.
    2 Sometimes.
    1 Hardly ever.
    0 Never.

Figure 3.1.5

The Mini Mental State Examination (adapted from Folstein, M.F., Robbins, L.N. and Helzer, J.E. (1983) *Archives of General Psychiatry*, **40,** 812). Cut-off point for probable cognitive impairment = 24

Patient name

Date of birth _____ Date of test _____

Section	Questions:	Max. points	Patient score
1 Orientation	**a)** Can you tell me today's (date)/(month)/(year)? Which (day of the week) is it today? Can you also tell me which (season) it is?	5	
	b) What city/town are we in? What is the (county)/(country)? What (building) are we in and on what (floor)?	5	
	(Score 1 for each correct answer)		
2 Registration	I should like to test your memory. (Examiner to name 3 common objects: e.g. "ball, car, man") Can you repeat the words I said? *(score 1 point for each word)* (repeat up to 6 trials until all three are remembered) (record number of trials needed here:)	3	
3 Attention & Calculation	**a)** From 100 keep subtracting 7 and give each answer: stop after 5 answers. (93 86 79 72 65). *Alternatively* **b)** Spell the word 'WORLD' backwards. (D__L__R__O__W).	5	
4 Recall	What were the three words I asked you to say earlier? *(Skip this test if all three objects were not remembered during registration test)*	3	
5 Language **Naming** **Repeating**	 Name these objects (show a watch) (show a pencil) Repeat the following: "no ifs, ands or buts"	 2 1	
6 Reading **Writing**	(show card or write "CLOSE YOUR EYES") Read this sentence and do what it says. Now can you write a short sentence for me?	 1 1	
7 Three stage command	(Present paper) Take this paper in your left (or right) hand, fold it in half, and put it on the floor.	3	
8 Construction	Will you copy this drawing please?	1	

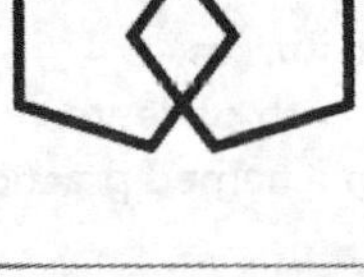

Total Score		30

Examiner

CASE STUDY 3.1.1

Philip Dodds, a recently retired journalist, is visited twice a week by a district nurse for care of a slow-healing foot wound. He is fairly incapacitated by the foot and is becoming quite isolated. He always offers the nurse an alcoholic drink, regardless of the time of day, and on a couple of occasions has appeared drunk himself. She suspects vascular problems are slowing the healing process and may be alcohol related. She feels embarrassed about broaching the subject of his drinking habits.

How would you advise her to proceed?

- Compile some evidence: work with her to list all the indicators suggesting that alcohol may be a problem for him: vascular disease, a job where alcohol problems are a high risk, entrenched drinking habits from recent working days, retirement allowing more time to drink, retirement and poor health leading to social isolation where drink becomes a comfort, drinking at all times of the day.
- Allow extra time for an appointment – given that he is isolated and often asking her to stay for a drink this should not be a problem.
- Ask for his assessment of the situation – encourage him to admit that his foot is not healing.
- Give factual information about vascular disease and explain that it can be alcohol related – say you've noticed that he drinks and probe a little more about his habits.
- Encourage him to fill in a drink diary – emphasize the assessment element of the diary and explain how this provides a baseline by which to decide whether alcohol plays a part.

CASE STUDY 3.1.2

A health centre is reviewing the care of patients who attend for regular depot anti-psychotic injections. At present the GPs tend to refer to the practice nurses all patients who they deem to be relatively stable. The nurses explain they allow a 5–10-minute appointment and their focus is on administering the injection: this is carried out by whichever practice nurse is available at the time. The onus is on the patient to arrange the next appointment. The patient is only referred back to the GP if their behaviour gives cause for concern.

What aspects should the review cover?

- System of referral.
- Provision of specific training for practice nurses.
- Introduction of concept of regular assessment and review of patient treatment.
- Forging links with primary and secondary services, setting up liaison systems.
- Instituting protocols for dealing with particular related issues.

How would you propose to achieve this?

- Carry out an audit to ascertain the number of patients and the primary and secondary services input for each.
- Hold a consensus group between GP and practice nurses to establish what constitutes appropriate referral.
- Establish the required knowledge base for practice nurses: about the illness, its treatment, the medication and side-effects, and support available in the community. Use secondary services to provide the necessary training and continuing support.
- Consider a regular liaison meeting with community psychiatric nurses.
- Hold a trial for using an assessment and review questionnaire with patients.
- Set down protocols for non-attendance, continuity of care from a named practice nurse, occulargyric crisis.

3.2 ANTI-PSYCHOTIC MEDICATION: ADMINISTRATION AND MANAGEMENT GUIDELINES

Nonspecialist nurses should not be expected to carry out duties related to psychiatric nursing – such as the administration of a depot anti-psychotic injection – without receiving background information about the condition and the drug treatment, instruction in the procedure, details about the patient's personal, medical and psychiatric history and professional support and advice from both GP and referring agency.

The Scope of Professional Practice, United Kingdom Central Council for Nursing, Midwifery and Health Visiting, 1992

Anti-psychotic medication and schizophrenia

Medication to treat psychotic symptoms has only been available since the 1950s. These drugs are often referred to as 'major tranquillizers' because of their sedating and calming effect and they are also, more accurately, called 'neuroleptics' and 'psychotropics', but the plain-speaking term of 'anti-psychotics' is most helpful because the primary effect is to counter the acute symptoms of a psychotic illness; the delusions, hallucinations and thought disorder of schizophrenia, for instance.

Other indications for treatment with anti-psychotic medication

Anti-psychotics are the drug of first choice in the treatment of schizophrenia.

They are also effective in treating mania, psychotic depression, acute agitation and confusional states – including those found in dementia – and in Tourette's syndrome.

Chemical group	Oral preparation	Depot preparation	Dose
Phenothiazines	Chlorpromazine Thioridazine Trifluoperazine	Fluphenazine deconoate (Modecate) Pipothiazine deconoate (Piportil)	12.5–100 mg weekly 50–10 mg weekly
Thioxanthines	Flupenthixol Clopenthixol	Flupenthixol deconoate (Depixol) Zuclopenthixol deconoate (Clopixol)	20–400 mg weekly 200–400 mg weekly
Butrophenones	Haloperidol Droperidol	Haloperidol deconoate (Haldol)	50–300 mg weekly
Benzamides	Sulpiride		
Diphenylbutyl piperidines	Pimozine		
Atypical	Clozapine Risperidone		

Table 3.2.1

Anti-psychotic medication

Figure 3.2.1

The Z-tracking technique

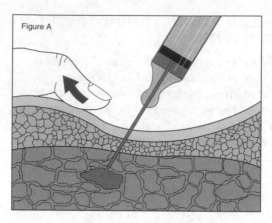

Figure A

- Using the thumb apply a shearing stress to the skin so that the skin and subcutaneous tissue slide over the underlying muscle. Inject through the displaced skin with a smooth action (Figure A).

- Do not allow the hilt of the needle to touch the skin as violent movement could cause the needle to break at the base.

- If resistance is felt, it probably indicates contact with the ilium and the needle should be retracted by 1/4 inch.

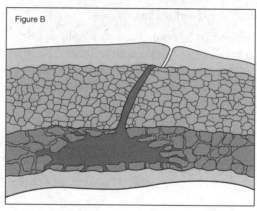

Figure B

- If any blood tracks alongside the needle it should be withdrawn and resited.

- As with all oily injections, it is important to ensure, by aspiration before injection, that inadvertent intravascular entry does not occur.

- After full depression of the plunger the needle should be withdrawn and the shearing force to the skin simultaneously released (Figure B).

How do they work?

Anti-psychotic medication works by interfering with the transmission of dopamine in the brain, achieved by blocking certain of the dopamine receptors.

How are they given?

Anti-psychotic medication may be given orally, by short-acting intramuscular or intravenous injection, or by long-acting intramuscular depot injection.

Depot administration

This drug therapy is usually continued long-term over many years, and is given every 1–5 weeks. The injection should only be given in the upper outer quadrant of the buttock and ideally should be alternated between left and right buttock each time to minimize local reactions. The Z-tracking technique of administration is recommended where the skin is pushed up and away from the injection site by the thumb and released just as the needle is withdrawn. This minimizes back-tracking or seepage of the drug.

The syringe plunger should be depressed at a slow rate because the oily nature of the product makes it slower and more painful to absorb. Careful attention needs to be paid to the injection site, which must be observed for inflammation, lumps under the skin, and haematoma. Local reactions may indicate a need for treatment change: a dose reduction or an increase in the time between injections. Always use the most concentrated form of the drug to ensure that the injected amount is as small as possible.

◄ *Key points*

Why use depot anti-psychotics?
- There is a lower relapse rate compared to oral preparations.
- Side-effects are minimized when a more constant level of medication is maintained in the bloodstream.
- Patient preference to remembering daily oral medication.
- Increases compliance.

Side-effects (SEs)

Side-effects are many and some are particularly unpleasant. Given this, it is not surprising that many patients are keen to reduce, or cease to take, their medication. However, it is important to weigh this against the devastating effects of untreated schizophrenia. Indeed, may patients, once reminded of their suffering during acute episodes of the illness, are loath to risk a return to that state. Between 30 and 40% of patients receiving regular depot injections will experience side-effects.

It is a cruel irony that it is often the side-effects of the medication that alert us to the fact that someone is suffering from a mental illness. The symptoms of shuffling gait, drooling mouth, sudden jerky movements and a constant restlessness are so easily misinterpreted as a psychiatric condition. It is often these manifestations that cause sufferers to be shunned or unfairly labelled 'mad', 'crazy' or dangerous.

Problems with medication compliance
Compliance problems with this patient group are common. Exploration of the cause(s) of resistance may clarify how best to facilitate treatment for individual patients.

Table 3.2.2

Side-effects of anti-psychotic medication

Side-effect type	Symptom	Treatment suggestions
Extra-pyramidal (EPS): Parkinsonian	Mostly affects those on high and sustained doses. Tremor, shuffling gait, muscle rigidity, mask-like facial expression	Consider dose reduction. Give prophylactic oral anti-cholinergics. Be aware that procylidene is abused for its 'buzz' and has a street value.
Dystonic	Abnormal muscle movements of face and body, drooling. Akinesia – limb weakness, muscle fatigue	Give oral anti-cholinergics.
Acute dystonic reactions	All the above plus: Oculargyro crisis (syndrome characterized by eyes rolling up and back) Retrocollis (head and neck forced back) Torticollis (head and neck forced to one side)	*This is a psychiatric emergency – proceeds to muscular and respiratory collapse.* Give stat. dose of IM anti-cholinergics, e.g. procyclidine 10 mg Refer for medication review.
Tardive dyskinesia (TD) Approximately 15% of patients on depot anti-psychotics are estimated to suffer from TD	Involuntary abnormal and bizarre body movements: orofacial (chewing and gurning) and of limb and trunk, appearing after approx. 3 months' treatment	Irreversible with no treatment: observe for early signs and reduce or cease medication. Once TD is entrenched it will worsen if dose is discontinued – perhaps because Parkinsonian SEs mask TD symptoms.
Akathisia	Continuous and distressing feeling of restlessness; pacing, rocking, fidgeting, 'the jitters'	Beta-blockers can help.
Anti-cholinergic	Dry mouth, constipation, blurred vision, nasal stuffiness, urinary hesitancy/retention	
Endocrine	Amenorrhea, infertility, impotence, lowered libido (male), breast enlargement (female), gynaeomastia (male breast development), galactorrhea (breast lactation: male and female).	
Gastrointestinal	Appetite increase, weight gain, anti-emetic	
Toxic	Phototoxicity (skin sensitivity to sun) and skin rashes Neuroleptic malignancy syndrome (relatively rare – but possibly underdiagnosed) Fever, muscle rigidity, fluctuating vital signs *Clozapine can cause agranulocytosis.*	Use sun block to avoid sunburn. *This is a psychiatric emergency – refer urgently to casualty department.* Once stable, requires psychiatric review. Regular monitoring of blood. If identified cease treatment. Requires psychiatric review.
Anti-adrenergic	Postural hypotension (blood pressure drops on standing – risk of falls) Sedation	Monitor blood pressure. Consider dose reduction.

Compliance problem	Trouble-shooting suggestions	Who to involve	
Medication side-effects – particularly those of a severe, socially disabling and enduring nature	• Take SEs seriously – acknowledgement alone can provide support. • Medication review. • Limit patient waiting time if akathisia is a problem. • Observe for early signs of SEs; use an assessment tool to monitor change over time.	• Refer to GP, suggest trying recommended medication for SEs. • Refer to psychiatrist. • Self-help groups, where sharing of common problems offers support and minimizes isolation.	**Table 3.2.3** Problems with medication compliance
Lack of insight – and thus a failure to recognize a need for the medication – leading to non-attendance	• Monitor non-attendance for depot; may be a sign of relapse. • Powers of persuasion! • Compulsory admission to hospital may be required.	• Involve the GP. • Involve the psychiatric team (CPN, SW, etc.). • Seek co-operation of a trusted friend or relative of the patient.	
Diagnosis resistance – to accepting the stigmatizing label of a severe and enduring mental illness, which the medication regime might come to represent	• Allow the patient to express their feelings. • Point out differences between their view and the reality of the disruption their unchecked symptoms have caused them.	• Patient advocacy groups such as MIND and SANE offer support and understanding. • Self-help groups such as NSF offer practical advice, provide group identity and build esteem.	
Influence of positive symptoms – delusional ideas, e.g. about being poisoned or interfered with, where side-effects make them feel bad, might compound suspicions	• Express your acceptance of the strength of their beliefs while maintaining yours; that they are unwell and need help. • Consider emergency referral.	• Involve the GP. • Involve the psychiatric team. • Emergency services (police, ambulance) might be required.	
Effect of negative symptoms – where inertia, lethargy and forgetfulness make it difficult to physically attend for appointments	• Try to fit the depot appointment in at a time to complement the structure of their day. • Refer for a medication review (newer anti-psychotics are more successful in countering negative symptoms).	• Discuss with the CPN or other mental health worker. • Refer to the GP. • Refer to the psychiatrist.	
Medication is prophylactic – when well, one resists taking preventive medication – consider how many of us fail to complete antibiotic courses once the acute symptoms disappear. N.B. Parallels drawn with diabetes are misleading: effects of omitting insulin are rapid and debilitating. Omitting depot anti-psychotic medication often makes the sufferer feel better for weeks or months before a breakdown is precipitated.	• Acknowledge the effort taken to continue with the medication regime. • Balance the pros of symptom control with the cons – try this exercise on paper with the patient.	• Discuss with the CPN or other mental health worker.	

CASE STUDY 3.2.1

The receptionist buzzes through to the practice nurse room in some state of agitation explaining that Eric Peebles, who was due his depot injection in your last appointment slot today, arrived early and jumped the queue of patients at the desk waiting to be booked in. He then paced about the reception area, demanded to be seen and when refused was verbally abusive and walked out. The receptionist is clearly upset, and expresses her belief that 'all of these schizophrenics should be in hospital, because they are dangerous'.'

How would you deal with the many issues that arise with this incident?

The receptionist's immediate distress:

- Sympathize and arrange to talk together after surgery.

The disturbed state of the patient (which you were unable to witness first-hand) – what possible causes for this behaviour might you consider?

- An outside event has precipitated his agitated state.
- He is responding to delusional ideas or auditory hallucinations.
- It is a sign of imminent relapse.
- He is experiencing acute akathisia, which makes waiting intolerable.

The missed depot injection:

- Make contact with the patient as soon as possible.
- Include the assistance of other disciplines if required.
- Ensure that the depot is given within the next day or so.

Prevention of a recurrence of this and similar incidents:

- Ensure that protocols exist and are known about for dealing with such incidents.
- Consider with the patient the best time and place for giving the depot.
- Assess for akathisia and if a problem refer for medication review.
- Discuss the inappropriateness of his behaviour and consider alternative strategies for him to make his feelings known in an acceptable way.

Provision of appropriate information/education for non-medical/nursing staff:

- Use material provided here to give clear information about schizophrenia, dispel myths etc.
- Have information leaflets about schizophrenia readily available in waiting areas.

CASE STUDY 3.2.2

Eva Chappell, who is physically disabled from brain damage following a suicide attempt 10 years ago, has received her depot injection – along with intensive physical nursing care – from the district nurses for 2 years. This has been a happy arrangement, which has worked well. However, she has recently experienced an increase in persecutory 'voices' and a community psychiatric nurse has begun to visit regularly and has taken over the depot administration. At a recent review by the psychiatrist her depot is increased. One day, when the district nurses make their routine daily visit to Eva, they find that she is drooling copiously from the mouth and her neck appears twisted back and to the side. The nurses are aware that the CPN attended earlier that day to give the first increased depot dose.

What might they suspect is happening?

- An oculargyric crisis.

What other signs and symptoms would confirm this?

- Limb weakness and rigidity, inability to speak, eyes rolling upwards and back.

How should they deal with the immediate clinical incident?

- Stay with the patient.
- Reassure the patient that you know what the matter is and can put it right quite quickly.
- Contact the GP urgently to administer the statutory dose of IM anti-cholinergic.
- If the GP or antidote medication is unavailable, get the patient to hospital for this procedure.

What implications does this hold for future safe practice?

- Develop protocol whereby administration of new prescriptions or increases in this medication are always undertaken at the surgery.
- Keep IM anti-cholinergic as a stock item.
- Liaise with the community psychiatric nurse to ensure that he/she is kept abreast of the incident and its outcome.

3.3 A–Z OF SUPPORT GROUPS AND MENTAL HEALTH ORGANIZATIONS

Action for ME

Action for ME provides information on symptoms, treatments and research to sufferers of ME, post-viral fatigue syndrome and chronic fatigue syndrome. The organization produces a comprehensive range of fact sheets covering all aspects of the illness. Sufferers of ME can join the organization and make use of counselling lines, therapy and welfare benefits advice and the journal *InterAction*. Action for ME has a website containing information on the condition.

Support and contact information
Address: PO Box 1302, Wells, BA5 1YE
Tel: 01749 670799
Fax: 01749 672561
E-mail: afme@afmeuk.demon.co.uk
Internet: http://www.afme.org.uk

AD/HD Support Groups UK

Attention Deficit Hyperactivity Disorder Family Support Groups UK promote awareness of AD/HD. The organization provides free information packs and advice for parents and professionals on issues relating to AD/HD. The organization requires a large stamped addressed envelope with all requests for their resources on hyperactivity.

Support and contact information
Helpline: 01373 826045/01380 726710
Address: 1a High Street, Dilton Marsh, Westbury, Wiltshire, BA13 4DL
Tel: 01373 826045
Fax: 01373 825158

Adfam National

Adfam National is a national registered charity, which works with the families and friends of people who misuse drugs. It offers a confidential telephone help-line service, training in family support skills and a variety of forms of information on drug and alcohol misuse and support. Publications include a newsletter detailing training, new resources and developments in the drug awareness/prevention field, and booklets for parents and partners on living with drug users. The organization also produces a recommended reading list of titles and resources not produced by themselves but which cover alcohol and substance misuse issues. The Alcohol Concern website is a further source of useful information.

Support and contact information

Address: 5th floor, Epworth House, 25 City Road, London,
              EC1Y 1AA
Tel: 020 7928 8900
Fax: 020 7256 6320
Internet: http://www.alcoholconcern.org.uk/

African Caribbean Mental Health Association

The African Caribbean Mental Health Association is a voluntary organization working with black people who experience mental health problems. The organization offers intervention services, such as psychotherapy, counselling and alternative therapies, legal services, advocacy and housing advice. The organization produces a newsletter and information about mental health issues.

Support and contact information

Address: 35–37 Electric Avenue, Brixton, London, SW9 8JP
Tel: 020 7737 3603
Fax: 020 7924 0126

Age Concern England

Age Concern is a national registered charity working with and for older people. They produce 45 fact sheets on topics of interest to older people, their carers and families and health professionals. Details of these can be found in the free publication list or by looking at the organizations excellent website. There are a large number of locally based Age Concern branches throughout the UK that provide some direct care services and an excellent source of local support and information for older people and their carers.

Support and contact information

Helpline: 0800 009966
Address: Astral House, 1268 London Road, London, SW6 4ER
Tel: 020 8765 7200
Fax: 020 8765 7211
E-mail: ace@ace.org.uk
Internet: http://www.ace.org.uk

Al-Anon Family Groups UK and Eire

Al-Anon Family Groups offers understanding and support for families and friends of problem drinkers, whether the person is still drinking or not. Alateen is part of Al-Anon aimed at young people aged 12–20 who have been affected by someone else's drinking, usually a parent. The organization provides meetings throughout the UK and Eire. Details can be obtained via one of the contact methods listed below. Al-Anon produce a wide range of leaflets and a variety of books and posters on alcohol issues. Details in the publications list available from the address below.

Support and contact information
Helpline: 020 7403 0888
Address: 61 Great Dover Street, London, SE1 4YF
Tel: 020 7403 0888
Fax: 020 7378 9910
E-mail: alanonuk@aol.com
Internet: http://www.hexnet.co.uk/alanon/

Alcoholics Anonymous

Alcoholics Anonymous (AA) is a voluntary fellowship of men and women who are alcoholics and who help each other to achieve and maintain sobriety by sharing experiences and giving mutual support. AA groups are autonomous and self-supporting that meet throughout the country each week. An AA group meets somewhere every night. The only requirement of people who attend is that they have a desire to stop drinking alcohol. The general office (contact number below) can provide details of times and locations. AA produce a wide range of books, pamphlets and information leaflets on the AA 12-step one-day-at-a-time approach to recovery from alcohol misuse.

Support and contact information
Helpline: Various helplines nationally.
Address: PO Box 1, Stonebow House, Stonebow, York YO1 2NJ
Tel: 01904 644026
Fax: 01904 629091
Internet: http://www.alcoholics-anonymous.org.uk

Alcohol Concern

Alcohol Concern is a national registered charity, which aims to reduce alcohol misuse in the UK and to provide services to people with alcohol problems and their families. The organization produce a range of publications, details of which are provided in their extensive publications list. In addition to books the organization offers leaflets, booklets, games, handbooks and project packs that can be used by school and college students. The organization's website (address below) is an additional source of information.

Support and contact information
Address: Waterbridge House, 32–36 Loman Street, London
               SE1 0EE
Tel: 020 7928 7377
Fax: 020 7928 4644
Internet: http://www.alcoholconcern.org.uk/

Alzheimer's Disease Society

The Alzheimer's Disease Society is a national membership organization working with and for people with dementia and their families. The organization has about 280 local branches and support groups, details of which can be found in local telephone directories. The society is able to provide information on Alzheimer's disease and the care of sufferers for carers and professionals. Local branches and the national helpline (see below) provide telephone support and give advice to families in need. The organization produces fact sheets and advice leaflets on various issues relating to dementia and the care of people with Alzheimer's disease. These include a number aimed at carers including 'How the GP can help', 'Services: who can help' and 'Carers: looking after yourself'. A number of publications are available in Polish, Cantonese and various Asian languages.

Support and contact information
Helpline: 0845 300 0336 (Mon–Fri, 8 am–6 pm)
Address: Gordon House, 10 Greencoat Place, London
             SW1P 1PH
Tel: 020 7306 0606
Fax: 020 7306 0808
E-mail: info@alzheimers.org.uk
Internet: http://www.alzheimers.org.uk

Anti-bullying Campaign

The Anti Bullying Campaign provides advice, support and information to bullied children and their parents on issues associated with bullying and methods of dealing with it. The organization produces free fact sheets and low-cost resource packs for parents and schools (£8.50) containing a variety of information leaflets, posters, questionnaires and role play materials.

Support and contact information
Helpline: 020 7378 1446
Address: 185 Tower Bridge Road, London SE1 2UF
Tel: 020 7378 1446
Fax: 020 7378 8374
Internet: http://www.ourworld.compuserve.com/homepages/Anti-
             Bullying

Association for Post-Natal Illness

The Association for Post-Natal Illness aims to help women who suffer from post-natal mental health problems. The organization provides clear, straightforward and supportive information on 'baby blues' and post-natal depression for women sufferers, family members and health workers.

Support and contact information
Helpline: 020 7386 0868
Address: 25 Jerdan Place, Fulham London SW6 1BE
Tel: 020 7386 0868
Fax: 020 7386 8885
E-mail: info@apni.org
Internet: http://www.apni.org.uk

Bristol Crisis Service for Women

Bristol Crisis Service for Women (BCSW) works to support women in distress. The organization produce a range of booklets on issues relating to self-injury and self-harm. As well as providing information, the organization offers direct help and support to women who self-injure through the helpline. BCSW also produces a training pack, *Working with People Who Self-injure*. Details of this and other publications can be found in the free publication list.

Support and contact information
Helpline: 0117 925 1119 (Fri and Sat 9 pm–12.30 am)
Address: PO Box 654, Bristol BS99 1XH
Tel: 0117 925 1119
E-mail: bcsw@womens-crisis-service.freeserve.co.uk
Internet: http://wwwusers.zetnet.co.uk/bcsw/

British Hypnotherapy Association

The British Hypnotherapy Association aims to maintain a register of competent, qualified practitioners of hypnotherapy. The organization can provide details of therapists working in your local area and a list of publications on hypnotherapy and its uses. Details of titles and costs are provided in the free publication list.

Support and contact information
Helpline: 020 7723 4443
Address: 67 Upper Berkeley Street, London W1H 7DH
Tel: 020 7723 4443

British Reflexology Association

The British Reflexology Association was founded in 1985. It is the representative body of people practising reflexology as a profession. The BRA publishes a members register, *Footprints*, a quarterly newsletter and an informative general information leaflet about reflexology and the British Reflexology Association. The Bayley School of Reflexology is the official teaching body of the Association. It offers a range of books, charts, videos and items of equipment on reflexology. Details of titles and costs are provided in the free publication list.

Support and contact information

Helpline:	01886 821207
Address:	Monks Orchard, Whitborne, Worcester WR6 5RB
Tel:	01886 821207
Fax:	01886 822017
E-mail:	bra@britreflex.co.uk
Internet:	http://www.brotreflex.co.uk

Carers National Association

Carers National Association helps carers to speak with a stronger voice. They provide information and advice on all aspects of caring to both carers and professionals. Carersline answers over 20 000 carers' enquiries each year. CNA's UK-wide network of offices and branches offer support to carers and provide feedback on local practices and policies towards carers. Carers National Association produces free and low-cost information booklets on practical, financial and legal issues for carers and professionals, including a number with a primary care focus.

Support and contact information

Helpline:	Carers' Line (Freephone) 0808 808 7777 (Mon–Fri, 12 noon and 2 pm–4 pm)
Address:	Ruth Pitter House, 20–25 Glasshouse Yard, London EC1A 4JT
Tel:	020 7490 8818
Fax:	020 7490 8824
Internet:	www.carersuk.demon.co.uk

Chinese Mental Health Association

The Chinese Mental Health Association is a voluntary organization that aims to help Chinese people who are sufferers of mental illness. The organization works to promote mental health awareness in the Chinese community and awareness of Chinese mental health issues amongst mainstream mental health providers. Services offered include professional assessments and counselling, a home support project and the *Chinese Mental Health Book*.

Support and contact information

Address:	Oxford House, Derbyshire Street, London E2 6HG
Tel:	020 7613 1008

The Compassionate Friends

The Compassionate Friends offer support to bereaved parents as well as to grandparents and siblings after the death of a child or children. The organization provides a national telephone helpline, group meetings, letter and a telephone contact for people who are grieving. The organization produces an information pack for professionals, a range of low-cost leaflets for bereaved families and a quarterly newsletter for subscribers. Details are available in the free publication list.

Support and contact information
Helpline: 0117 953 9639
Address: 53 North Street, Bristol BS3 1EN
Tel: 0117 966 5202
Fax: 0117 966 5202
E-mail: info@tcf.org.uk

Counsel for Involuntary Tranquillizer Addiction (CITA)

CITA is a registered charity that has been established for 10 years. Its main aim is to help people addicted to prescription benzodiazepine tranquillizers. The organization can provide information and advice to people with tranquillizer addiction, mainly through a national telephone help line. CITA produces a range of publications related to tranquillizer addiction and ways of withdrawing from their use. These include free leaflets and books and tapes, for which a small charge is made.

Support and contact information
Helpline: 0151 949 0102
Address: Cavendish House, Brighton Road, Waterloo, Liverpool L22 5NG
Tel: 0151 747 9629 (Office)
Fax: 0151 949 0102
Internet: http://www.liv.ac.uk/~csunit/community/cita.htm

Cruse Bereavement Care

Cruse Bereavement Care is the largest bereavement charity in the UK, with 180 local branches. It offers help to people bereaved by death in any way, whatever their age, nationality or belief. Cruse's help includes a free counselling service for bereaved people, opportunities for contact with others through bereavement support groups and advice or information on practical matters. It is personal and confidential help backed by a wide range of publications. Bereaved people who wish to speak to a counsellor on the telephone can use the national telephone helpline. Cruse Bereavement Care produces an extensive range of leaflets, an information pack, and books on bereavement and grief. Details of titles and costs are available in the free Cruse Mail Order catalogue.

Support and contact information
Helpline: 0354 585 565 (afternoons and evenings 7 days a week) or 020 8940 4818 for details of local Cruse branch

Address: Cruse House, 126 Sheen Road, Richmond, Surrey
             TW9 1UR
Tel: 020 8940 4818
Fax: 020 8940 7638

Depressives Anonymous (Fellowship of)

Depression is a very common mental health problem that is often presented in primary care settings. The Fellowship of Depressives (FOD) is a self-help and mutual aid organization that provides information, advice and support for depression sufferers and for their relatives and friends. The FOD produce leaflets including *Ten rules for coping with panic*, *Depression – a self-help guide* and *Helpful thoughts for individuals and groups*.

Support and contact information
Address: Box FDAI, c/o Self-help Nottingham,
             Ormiston House, 32–36 Pelham Street,
             Nottingham NG1 2EG
Tel: 01702 43 38 38
Fax: 01702 43 38 43

Depression Alliance

The Depression Alliance is run by people who have experienced depression themselves. It is a national registered charity and is able to provide information, support and understanding to other people who are depressed and to their carers. The organization co-ordinates local support groups, a pen friend scheme, and produces a variety of information sheets on depression and its treatment.

Support and contact information
Address: 35 Westminster Bridge Road, London SE1 7JB
Tel: 020 7633 0557
Fax: 020 7633 0559
E-mail: hg@depressionalliance.org.uk
Internet: http://www.depressionalliance.org.uk

Drinkline

The organization will provide information about alcohol to anybody who needs it. Helpline staff can also advise callers on where to go for help and will supply self-help materials where appropriate.

Support and contact information
Address: Weddel House, 7th Floor, 13–14 West Smithfield,
             London EC1A 9DL
Tel: 020 7320202 (UK helpline Mon–Fri, 11 am–11 pm)

0990 133480 (Asian line Mon 1–8 pm in Hindi, Urdu, Gujerati and Punjabi)

Eating Disorders Association

The Eating Disorders Association is a national charity providing information, help and support for people affected by eating disorders and, in particular, anorexia and bulimia nervosa. The organization can provide details of local groups and runs a number of help-lines for young people and adults who wish to talk to somebody about an eating disorder. The EDA produce a range of training materials and publications to help suffers and professionals understand eating disorders. Details are provided on the publication list, which is available on request.

Support and contact information

Helpline:	01603 621 414 (week days, 9 am–6.30 pm)
Youthline:	01603 765 050 (up to 18 years of age. Weekdays 4–6 pm)
Recorded info:	0906 302 0012 (calls cost 50p per minute)
Address:	1st floor, Wensum House, 103 Prince of Wales Road, Norwich NR1 1DW
Tel (admin.):	01603 619090
Fax:	01603 664915
E-mail:	info@edauk.com
Internet:	http://www.edauk.com

First Steps to Freedom

First Steps to Freedom is a registered charity which aims to provide practical help to people who experience phobias, obsessional compulsive disorders, those with general anxiety, panic attacks, anorexia and bulimia and people who wish to come off tranquillizers. The organization offers a confidential helpline, telephone self-help groups, counselling and befriending and a range of publications and relaxation audio tapes.

Support and contact information

Helpline:	01926 851608 (10 am–10 pm every day)
Address:	7 Avon Court, Scholl Lane, Kenilworth, Warwickshire CV8 2GX
Tel:	01926 864473
Fax:	01926 864473/0870 1640567
E-mail:	lesley@firststeps.demon.co.uk
Internet:	http://www.firststeps.demon.co.uk/

The Foundation for the Study of Infant Deaths

The Foundation for the Study of Infant Deaths raises funds for research into sudden infant death syndrome as well as infant care and health. The

Foundation provides a telephone helpline, befriending and support for bereaved families following sudden infant death. FSID produces and distributes an extensive range of low-cost information resources on prevention of and response to cot death. These include leaflets, videos, fact files and information packs. Details of titles and costs are provided in the free publication list. The FSID website is also a useful and easily accessible source of information.

Support and contact information
Helpline: 24-hour cot death helpline: 020 7233 2090
Address: Artillery House, 11–19 Artillery Row, London SW1P 1RT
Tel: 020 7222 8001
Fax: 020 7222 8002
E-mail: fsid@sids.org.uk
Internet: http://www.sids.org.uk/fsid/

GamCare

GamCare is the National Association for Gambling Care, Education and Training. The organization aims to provide information, advice and practical help to reduce the social impact of gambling and address the needs of those who have a gambling dependency. GamCare has a national telephone helpline (0845 6000 133), a network of members, can offer face-to-face counselling and provides training and publications about gambling dependency. The organization produces a number of resources specifically aimed at young people and students. Information is also available through the GamCare website (address below).

Support and contact information
Helpline: 0845 6000 133 (Mon–Fri, 10 am–10 pm)
Address: Suite 1, Catherine House, 25–27 Catherine Place,
                Westminster, London SW1E 6DU
Tel: 020 7233 8988
Fax: 020 7233 8977
E-mail: director@gamcare.org.uk
Internet: http://www.gamcare.org.uk

Hearing Voices Network

Hearing Voices Network is a voluntary organization that helps set up self-help groups, which allows 'voice hearers' to explore their experiences in a secure, confidential way. The organization produces information including *Voices* magazine and an information pack. The magazine provides useful insights into people's experiences of 'voice hearing'.

Support and contact information
Helpline: 0161 228 3896 (10 am–3 pm – answer machine at
                other times)

Address: Dale House, 35 Dale Street, Manchester M1 2HF
Tel: 0161 228 3896

Huntington's Disease Association

Huntington's disease, also known as Huntington's chorea, is a hereditary disease caused by a genetic defect. Symptoms appear in early middle age and include jerky involuntary movements, behavioural changes and a progressive dementia. The Huntington's Disease Association aims to provide care, advice, support and education to people whose lives are affected by Huntington's disease. The organization also aims to educate health professionals working with people who have Huntington's disease. The organization produces a range of fact sheets and videos about Huntington's disease, as well as a low-cost information pack for professionals.

Support and contact information
Address: PO Box 35, Liverpool L36 6RQ
Tel: 020 7223 7000

Hyperactive Children's Support Group (HACSG)

The Hyperactive Children's Support Group is a voluntary organization that supports parents with children who have hyperactivity and attention deficit disorders. The organization provides information to care professionals who have an interest in these problems and encourages research into the conditions. HACSG produces a resource pack for professionals and is able to provide articles and an information leaflet about hyperactivity as a condition of childhood. The HACSG website is a further source of information on the topic of hyperactivity.

Support and contact information
Address: 71 Whyke Lane, Chichester, West Sussex PO19 2LD
Tel: 01903 725182
Fax: 01903 734726
E-mail: hacsg@hyperactive.force9.co.uk
Internet: Http://www.hyperactive.force9.co.uk

The Institute for the Study of Drug Dependence

The Institute for the Study of Drug Dependence (ISDD) is the national drug information service for the UK. Since 1968 it has collected and disseminated information on all aspects of drug misuse. Information can be provided on all types of misusable drugs, legal and illegal, but not alcohol or tobacco. The publications department of the organization produces a wide range of books, leaflets and other resources. Catalogues and details of services are available on request. The ISDD website is a source of useful information.

Support and contact information
Address: 32–36 Loman Street, London SE1 0EE
Tel: 020 7928 1211
Fax: services@isdd.co.uk
Internet: http://www.isdd.co.uk

Manic Depression Fellowship

The Manic Depression Fellowship helps people with manic depression/ bipolar disorder and those who care for them. The organization produces a range of fact sheets, books and information packs that aim to educate the public and care professions. There are local MDF self-help groups throughout the UK, details of which are available from the main contact number below.

Support and contact information
Address: 8–10 High Street, Kingston upon Thames, Surrey KT1
1EY Tel: 020 8974 6550
Fax: 020 8974 6600

The Mental Health Foundation

The Mental Health Foundation is a registered charity concerned with both mental health problems and learning disability. The organization seeks to play a role in raising awareness mental health issues and in pioneering new approaches to the prevention, treatment and care of people who experience mental illness or have learning disabilities. The foundation produces a series of booklets for those wanting to know more about mental health problems. The website is an excellent source of information and includes reports about primary care issues.

Support and contact information
Helpline: 08456 105050 (dial-and-listen information service only)
Address: 20–21 Cornwall Terrace, London NW1 4QL
Tel: 020 7535 7400
Fax: 020 7535 7474
E-mail: mhf@mhf.org.uk
Internet: http://www.mhf.org.uk

MIND

MIND is a national, voluntary sector mental health organization working for everyone experiencing mental distress. MIND campaigns for the right to lead an active and valued life in the community. It offers its services through regional offices and local organizations. MIND provides a national information line, a legal network, an extensive publications list, a bi-monthly magazine *OpenMind*, conferences, training and a range of community-based services for people with mental health problems. Information on all aspects of mental health can be obtained by ringing the MindinfoLine (details below), or from the extensive range of publications that are available free or at low cost. The Mind website (address below) is a further source of information.

Support and contact information

Address: 15–19 Broadway, Stratford, London E15 4BQ

Tel: 020 8522 1728 (if in London), 0345 660 163 (if outside London) (Mon–Fri, 9.15 am–4.45 pm)

Internet: http://www.MIND.org.uk

National Phobics Society

The National Phobics Society is a national registered charity that provides support, information and guidance to sufferers of all anxiety-based disorders, including obsessive compulsive disorder, body dysmorphic disorder, general anxiety, panic attacks, agoraphobia, social phobia and other specific phobias. The organization provides telephone counselling for members, self-help groups and self-help literature. This includes the NPS *Guide to Understanding Anxiety* and a range of fact sheets on anxiety.

Support and contact information

Helpline: Members only – phone general enquiries for details

Address: Zion Centre, Royce Road, Hulme, Manchester M15 5SQ

Tel: 0161 227 9862

E-mail: natphob.soc@good.co.uk

Internet: http://www.good.co.uk/national-phobics-society

National Schizophrenia Fellowship

National Schizophrenia Fellowship is a voluntary organization that aims to improve the lives of people affected by schizophrenia and other severe mental disorders. NSF provides support services and a range of publications (details in publications list) on issues relating to schizophrenia. NSF run relative support groups throughout the UK. The NSF websites are also a useful source of information.

Support and contact information

Helpline: 020 8974 6814 (Week days, 10 am–3 pm)

Address: 28 Castle Street, Kingston, Surrey KT1 1SS

Tel: 020 8547 3937

Fax: 020 8547 3862

E-mail: info@nsf.org.uk

Internet: Adults/professionals – http://www.nsf.org.uk

                    Young people – http://www.at-ease.nsf.org.uk

No Panic

No Panic is a voluntary, charitable organization whose aims are to aid the relief and rehabilitation of those people suffering from panic attacks, phobias, obsessive compulsive disorders and other anxiety related illnesses. No Panic provides confidential telephone help lines to sufferers and their families, raises public and professional awareness of phobic illnesses and produces a range of booklets and information packs on anxiety related illnesses.

Support and contact information
Helpline: 01952 590545
Address: 93 Brands Farm Way, Telford, Shropshire TF3 2JQ
Tel: 01952 590005 (general enquiries)
Fax: 01952 270962

Overeaters Anonymous

Overeaters Anonymous is a fellowship of men and women who are recovering from compulsive overeating using a twelve-step programme based on the Alcoholics Anonymous approach. Overeating can take many forms, including bingeing, starving, dieting, purging and eating excessively. They are all seen as being concerned with food and weight control. The organization produces a range of its own leaflets and books (details in the literature order form), which are available at various costs.

Support and contact information
Address: PO Box 19, Stretford, Manchester M32 9EB
Tel: 07000 784985

Parkinson's Disease Society of the United Kingdom

Parkinson's disease is a progressive neurological disorder in which an affected individual experiences tremors, rigidity and slowness of movement as a result of a brain disorder. The Parkinson's Disease Society is a registered charity founded in 1969. The aim of the society is to help individuals, and their relatives, with the problems arising from Parkinson's disease, to collect and disseminate information on the disease and to encourage and provide funds for research into Parkinson's disease. The society produces a publications list detailing an extensive range of leaflets, booklets, guides, information packs and videos written for patients, carers, students and educators.

Support and contact information
Address: 22 Upper Woburn Place, London WC1H 0RA

PMS Help

PMS Help is a registered charity offering educational and self-help materials and postal support to sufferers of premenstrual syndrome (PMS) and post-natal depression (PND), as well as their families and colleagues. The organization seeks to assist the medical profession and health professionals in understanding PMS and PND and supports research into these common, but often untreated, problems. PMS Help produces a range of free and low-cost leaflets, booklets, an award-winning video and a guide to treatment options. Details and prices are available in the publication leaflet.

Support and contact information
Address: PO Box 83, Hereford HR4 8YG

Premenstrual Society (PREMSOC)

The Premenstrual Society aims to give information and support to individuals about the physical and emotional features of premenstrual syndrome, as well as to people who experience period pain and dysmenorrhoea. PREMSOC provides education courses on PMS and can help individuals and organizations wishing to start self-help groups. PREMSOC produces a wide variety of leaflets on aspects of premenstrual syndrome.

Support and contact information
Address: PO Box 429, Addlestone, Surrey KT15 1DZ
Tel: 01932 872560 (for professionals/admin. use only)

The Princess Royal Trust for Carers

The Princess Royal Trust for Carers provides help, support and information for informal carers. The Princess Royal Trust for Carers has helped to establish sixty carers' centres across the UK, which provide local information, practical help, advocacy, emotional support, social events and access to respite care for all carers. The trust produces educational resources, including *Taken for granted – a survey of carers needs and outcomes, How to get GPs to recognize carers and projects that support them* (7.5 minute video) and *Too much to take – a report on young carers and bullying.*

Support and contact information
Address: 142 Minories, London EC3N 1LB
Tel: 020 7480 7788
Fax: 020 7481 4729
E-mail: info@carers.org.uk
Internet: http://www.carers.org.uk

Psychiatric Information Foundation UK (PIF-UK)

The Psychiatric Information Foundation (UK) is part of the Psychiatric Education Fund based in Norway. Both organizations aim to contribute to greater understanding of and openness towards psychiatric illness. PIF is an independent organization, directing its information towards people who experience mental health problems, their families, care professionals and the general public. The organization produces a range of high-quality, low-cost educational resources, including booklets and teaching packs, on illnesses such as schizophrenia, mania and depression, anxiety and eating disorders.

Support and contact information
Tel: 01865 552787
Fax: 01865 552787
E-mail: pif-uk@btinternet.com

RELATE (National Marriage Guidance)

RELATE provides counselling and psychosexual therapy to couples working in 128 centres in England, Wales and Northern Ireland. The organization produces a series of informative guides, which include *Welcome to Relate, Better Relationships, Sex in Loving Relationships, Starting Again, Second Families, Stop Arguing, Start Talking* and *Loving in Later Life*.

Support and contact information
Address: Herbert Gray College, Little Church Street,
                Rugby CV21 3AP
Tel: 01788 57324111
Fax: 01788 535007
E-mail: info@national.relate.org.uk

RELEASE

RELEASE is a national voluntary organization working to provide a range of services dedicated to meeting the health, welfare and legal needs of drug users and those who live and work with them. The organization specializes in drugs law and campaigns for changes in legislation relating to drugs. It produces a range of excellent, low-cost booklets, leaflets, and legal fact sheets on a range of drugs and drug-related issues. Staff are also available to provide advice on drug-related issues to individual callers, via the 24-hour helplines.

Support and contact information
Helpline: 020 7729 9904
Schools helpline: 0808 800 8000
Address: 388 Old Street, London EC1V 9LT
Tel: 020 7729 9904
Fax: 020 7729 2599
E-mail: info@release.org.uk
Internet: http://www.release.org.uk

Re-Solv

Re-Solv, The Society for the Prevention of Solvent and Volatile Substance Abuse, is the only organization in the UK solely concerned with volatile substance abuse prevention. The organization produces a range of educational and training information in booklet, video and leaflet form. These include an information pack for care professionals. Details of titles and costs are provided in the free publications list. The organization adopts a campaigning and educational approach to the problems associated with solvent abuse.

Support and contact information
Helpline: 0808 800 2345 (National freephone)
Address: 30a High Street, Stone, Staffs ST15 8PT
Tel: 01785 817885
Fax: 01785 813205
E-mail: information@re-solve.org.uk

Royal College of Psychiatrists

The Royal College of Psychiatrists (RCP) is the representative body of medically qualified psychiatrists. The RCP provides a broad range of educational information packs, checklists and fact sheets on mental health and illness topics, as well as books and audio tapes. These are useful for patient education and support. The range of publications is available at low cost, with a number of publications also available free on the RCP website.

Support and contact information
Address: 17 Belgrave Square, London SW1X 8PG
Tel: 020 7235 2351
Fax: 020 7245 1231
Internet: http://www.rcpsych.ac.uk

Samaritans

The Samaritans is a UK charity, founded in 1953, which exists to provide confidential emotional support to any person who is suicidal or despairing and to increase public awareness of issues surrounding suicide and depression. The service is provided 24 hours every day by trained volunteers. There are over 200 local branches in the UK and Ireland. A text phone service is available for deaf and hearing-impaired people.

Support and contact information
Helpline: 0345 909090
Address: 10 The Grove, Slough, Berkshire SL1 1QP
Tel: 01753 532713 (office/admin.)
Fax: 01753 775787
Internet: http://www.mentalhelp.net/samaritans

SANDS – Stillbirth and Neonatal Death Society

SANDS provides support for bereaved parents and their families when their baby dies at or soon after birth. The key elements of that support are a national telephone helpline service, a UK-wide network of self-help groups run by and for bereaved parents and information and publications for bereaved parents and health care professionals.

Support and contact information
Helpline: 020 7436 5881
Address: 28 Portland Place, London W1N 4DE
Tel: 020 7436 7940
Fax: 020 7436 3715

SANELINE

Saneline is a national registered charity offering telephone helpline services and various publications containing up to date information on aspects of mental health and mental disorder. Saneline operators offers emotional and crisis support to people with mental health problems, their families and friends. The SANE website is a source of additional information.

Support and contact information
Helpline: 0345 678000 (12 noon–2 am every day)
Address: 1st floor, Cityside House, 40 Adler Street,
                London E1 1EE
Tel: 020 7375 1002
Fax: 020 7375 2162
Internet: http://www.mkn.co.uk/help/charity/sane/index

Scottish Council on Alcohol

The Scottish Council on Alcohol is Scotland's national alcohol charity. The SCA aims to reduce alcohol misuse and to promote healthier life styles through education. The organization's main activities are training, education, advice and information provision and the co-ordination of a network of 28 affiliated agencies. The Scottish Council on Alcohol publishes a wide range of educational and self-help materials. These include fact sheets, posters and leaflets as well as books. Details of titles and costs are found in the publications list, which is available on request.

Support and contact information
Address: 166 Buchanan Street, Glasgow G1 2NH
Tel: 0141 333 9677
Fax: 0141 333 1606
E-mail: sca@clara.net

Seasonal Affective Disorders Association (SAD)

The SAD Association is a voluntary organization and registered charity that works to inform the public and health professions about seasonal affective disorder and supports and advises sufferers of the illness. It produces a comprehensive information pack (£5) and a free basic information leaflet on SAD. The organization also provides a help and advice line.

Support and contact information
Helpline: 01903 814942
Address: PO Box 989, Steyning, West Sussex BN44 3HG
Tel: 01903 814942
Fax: 01903 879939
Internet: http://www.sada.org.uk

Sudden Death Support Association

The Sudden Death Support Association is an organization run by and for people who have experienced a sudden death regardless of the circumstances of death. The organization can put the recently bereaved in contact with a volunteer who has been through a similar experience in order that the bereaved person has someone to whom they can directly relate to about their loss. The organization produces a free information leaflet, available on request.

Support and contact information
Helpline: 01189 790790 (Answer phone – calls returned in 24 hours)
Address: Chapel Green House, Chapel Green, Wokingham, Berks RG40 3ER
Tel: 01189 790790

Survivors Speak Out

Survivors Speak Out is a network of groups and individuals who are 'survivors' of the psychiatric system. The organization provides information about mental health self-advocacy and the user involvement/survivor movement. It seeks to provide and improve contact between users/ex-users of psychiatric services.

Support and contact information
Helpline: N/A. Phone main number to obtain details of local group.
Address: 34 Osnaburgh Street, London NW1 3ND
Tel: 020 7916 5473

Triumph over Phobia (TOP UK)

TOP UK are a network of structured self-help groups run by lay volunteers for phobia/OCD sufferers. Leaflets available – an SAE is required.

Support and contact information
Address: PO Box 1831, Bath BA1 4YW
Tel: 01225 330353

Vietnamese Mental Health Services

The Vietnamese Mental Project was established in 1989, following research into mental health problems amongst Vietnamese people in London. The project now provides services for Vietnamese people with mental health difficulties and their families living in London and beyond. The aims of the renamed VMHS are to increase access to adequate and appropriate health and social care for all Vietnamese people and to provide a culturally sensitive service. The VMHS provides outreach, counselling and drop in services, supported accommodation for Vietnamese people and training/education about mental health issues for Vietnamese people, about Vietnamese cultures and beliefs in mental health for non-Vietnamese professionals.

Support and contact information
Address: 49 Effra Road, Units 21 and 23, Brixton, London
                  SW2 1BZ
Tel: 020 7733 7646/6418
Fax: 020 7274 1373

Wales Mind Cymru

Mind Cymru campaigns for the rights of people who experience mental distress to be treated with respect, given equal access to services and opportunities in the community and to have more control of the care and treatment they receive. There is a network of over 20 independent Mind associations in Wales that work with local communities. Services include drop-in centres, supported housing, outreach work and befriending services.

Support and contact information
MindInfoLine: 0345 660163 (Mon–Fri, 9.15 am–4.45 pm)
Address: Mind Cymru, Third Floor, Quebec House, Castlebridge,
                  Cowbridge Road East, Cardiff CF11 9AB.
Tel: 029 2039 5123
Fax: 029 2022 1189
Internet: http://www.mind.org.uk/cymru

Women's Aid

Women's Aid provides support and services for women and children experiencing physical, sexual or emotional abuse in their homes. WAFE is the national organization that supports and resources the English network of 214 local refuge projects. There are other Women's Aid Federations in Scotland, Wales and Northern Ireland. WAFE provides a confidential national helpline, information and resources for local refuges, consultancy and support and training services to agencies working with women and children experiencing violence.

Support and contact information
Tel: 0117 963 3542

Young Minds

Young Minds is a national registered charity, which aims to raise public awareness of the mental health needs of children, young people and their families. The organization campaigns to ensure that social and health policies take account of the mental health needs of children and young people. Young Minds produces a range of information/education publications.

Support and contact information
Helpline: 0345 626376 (Parents information service)
Address: 22a Boston Place, London, NW1 6ER
                or
                2nd floor, 102–108 Clerkenwell Road,
                London EC1M 5SA
Tel: 020 7724 7262/020 7336 8445 (office)
Fax: 020 7723 5968

The Zito Trust

The Zito Trust is a registered charity focusing on improving the provision of community care for people with severe mental illness. The organization seek to raise the public's awareness of the needs of people with severe mental illness and their carers. The Zito Trust produces a newsletter, *ZT Monitor*, and regular reports on aspects of mental disorder.

Support and contact information
Address: 16 Castle Street, Hay-on-Wye, Hereford HR3 5AR
Tel: 01497 820011
Fax: 01497 820011
E-mail: zito@cs.com

GLOSSARY OF PSYCHIATRIC TERMS AND ABBREVIATIONS

Acute admission is a term used to refer to a person's admission to a psychiatric ward or unit, usually for assessment of their disturbed mental state or to manage a crisis situation. This is in contrast to a respite admission or admission to a rehabilitation unit, which tend to occur with more planning and no apparent crisis.

Addiction is a psychological or physiological over-dependence on a drug. Originally the term was used to refer only to physiological dependence; here, the drug altered the biochemistry of the person. The distinction between physiological and psychological dependence is often difficult to establish, leading to the broader use of the term.

Advocacy is the representation of a service user's interests by another (the advocate) in order to improve their situation. Citizen advocacy is a widely used form of advocacy in mental health settings. It involves an unpaid lay person developing an advocacy relationship with a service user in order to act as a spokesperson and to represent their interests and wishes.

Affect is a term that is often used interchangeably with emotion, feeling and mood. It is, however, used differently from mood to describe the general quality of a person's emotional response in a particular situation. Assessment reports may comment on or describe, for example, the appropriateness of a person's affect in terms of how 'normal' or acceptable it was in the particular situation.

Affective disorder is an umbrella term used to describe mood-related conditions. Depression and anxiety are affective disorders.

Agitation is a physical symptom. The term is used to describe excessive, anxiety-driven physical activity or behaviour the main quality of which is restlessness.

Aggression is a general term used to describe behaviour that involves hostility or attack. The term is often used loosely and doesn't necessarily indicate that a person is or has been physically violent – see also **de-escalation**.

Agranulocytosis is a disorder in which there is a marked decrease or absence of white blood cells (neutrophils) as a result of damage to the bone marrow caused by toxic drugs. This leaves the body defenceless against bacterial invasion. The symptoms of agranulocytosis are a sore, ulcerated throat and pyrexia, leading rapidly to prostration and death. Treatment is by administration of large doses of antibiotics and later transfusion of white blood cells.

Akathisia is the pattern of involuntary movements induced by the use of some anti-psychotic medications. People with akathisia complain of a continuous and distressing feeling of restlessness and involuntary tremors in their limbs manifested in fidgeting, pacing and rocking, which is beyond the conscious control of the sufferer. Anti-cholinergic medication, such as procyclidine, can help to reduce akathisia.

Alcoholism is an extreme physical and psychological addiction resulting from excessive consumption of alcohol over a relatively long period of time. Alcoholism has a variety of medical consequences as well as social and psychological difficulties (see Section 2.5, pp. 57–72).

Anorexia nervosa is a recognized eating disorder, mostly experienced by young women. Sufferers starve themselves or use other means, such as laxatives and exercise, to reduce their weight. People with anorexia nervosa tend to have a false perception of their bodies as being 'fat' (see Section 2.7, pp. 82–90).

Anti-cholinergic medication, such as procyclidine, inhibits the action of acetylcholine. Many anti-psychotic medications provoke side-effects – particularly **extra-pyramidal symptoms** – such as severe movement disorders, **Parkinsonian symptoms** and muscular dysfunction, as well as dry mouth and blurred vision, which are relieved by anticholinergic medication.

Anti-psychiatry is an umbrella term used to describe the range of theories and perspectives that see *mental illness* as a myth and the psychiatric system and approach to treatment of mental illness as oppressive and disempowering to the individual. Anti-psychiatry theories are associated with theorists such as R.D. Laing and Thomas Szasz and have developed from the 1960s onwards. It has led to the medical model of mental illness being challenged by social approaches and has been an important element of the self-help advocacy and 'survivor' movement. The central claim that mental illness is a myth is now largely rejected.

Anti-psychotic medication is a group of drugs that are used to treat severe and enduring psychotic mental illness or, in small doses, to treat anxiety. Antipsychotic medication includes phenothiazines (such as chlorpromazine), butyrophenones (such as haloperidol), thioxantheses such as (flupenthixol) and clopixol. Many antipsychotic medications have significant and unpleasant side-effects (Section 3.2, pp. 127–133).

Anxiety is the feeling of apprehension and fear caused by the anticipation of danger or loss of control (see Section 2.4, pp. 48–56).

Anxiolytic medication is used to treat anxiety-based disorders. Formerly known as minor tranquillizers, examples include diazepam, lorazepam and temazepam (see Section 2.4, pp. 48–56).

Apathy is the detached or indifferent quality of a person's behaviour or the loss of interest or ability to feel pleasure that can be a feature of depressive disorder or the negative symptoms of schizophrenia.

An **art therapist** is a trained psychotherapist, usually employed with a statutory health or social services setting, who uses art activities as a therapeutic vehicle for the expression and interpretation of psychological distress and problems that the individual cannot articulate verbally. Art therapy is usually conducted through one-to-one sessions, though some therapists also offer art therapy in group settings.

An **approved social worker (ASW)** is a specially qualified social worker who is employed by a local authority in order to co-ordinate Mental Health Act assessments. By law, an ASW must be involved in the decision to compulsorily detain a person in a psychiatric unit.

Athetoid movements are involuntary, recurring writhing movements of the hands, face and/or tongue. Athetosis can be the result of a cerebral lesion or can be a consequence of withdrawing phenothiazines or using medication to treat Parkinsonism.

Auditory hallucinations are often referred to as 'voices'. Individuals who experience auditory hallucinations have the sensory impression that they can hear a person or people speaking to or about them, or they hear some other form of sound, when there is no apparent basis for this in the external environment. There is nobody there but the person hears sound(s) that appear to come from the external environment (i.e. they are not the person 'hearing' their own thoughts). Auditory hallucinations are characteristic of psychotic disorders such as schizophrenia but can also be experienced by physical disorders of the brain, by substance misuse or sensory deprivation, excessive fatigue and stress.

Behavioural therapy is a form of psychotherapy that seeks to change maladaptive (abnormal) patterns of behaviour through the use of classical and operant conditioning techniques that make use of positive and negative reinforcers of behaviour. Behaviour therapy is commonly used to help people overcome compulsions and phobias.

Beta-blockers are drugs, such as propranolol, that are used to control abnormal heart rhythms, treat angina and reduce blood pressure. They may be used to treat the physical symptoms of people who experience high levels of anxiety.

Bi-polar affective disorder is another term for manic depressive psychosis (see Section 2.2, pp. 25–33).

Blunted affect is a disturbance in **affect** that is characterized by the flat or reduced intensity of emotional expression. It is a feature of schizophrenia and depressive disorders.

Bulimia nervosa is an eating disorder characterized by repeated episodes of 'binge' eating followed by misuse of laxatives or other means to expel the food that has been ingested. Bulimia nervosa usually co-exists with depressive disorder, guilt and low self-esteem (see Section 2.7, pp. 82–90).

Butrophenones are a group of chemically related drugs, such as haloperidol, droperidol and benperidol, that are use to treat the symptoms of psychosis.

Care in the community refers to the provision of care services and social support to people living in non-institutional, domestic settings in the community. The term is often associated with the policy-driven shift away from providing people with chronic or enduring mental health problems with in-patient care in large psychiatric hospitals that occurred in the late 1980s.

The Care Programme Approach (CPA) was an attempt to provide integrated, co-ordinated care for users of mental health services. it was introduced in the early 1990s and was used throughout statutory mental health services. The CPA was based on the development of an explicit after-care programme, co-ordinated by a key worker, in which the specific inputs and responsibilities of all professionals involved with a service user were outlined.

Catatonia is a state of stupor in which the person becomes mute, adopts bizarre postures or experiences almost complete psychomotor (physical) retardation. Catatonia is a rarely seen symptom of schizophrenia.

Chlorpromazine is the phenothiazine medication that is commonly used in the treatment of schizophrenia and mania.

Choroid movements are jerky involuntary movements that can affect the head, face and limbs. They are usually due to disease of the basal ganglia but can result from drugs used to treat parkinsonism or the withdrawal of phenothiazines. Choroid movements are also characteristic of Huntington's chorea.

Chronic means 'long lasting' and is used to indicate the enduring, ongoing nature of an individual's condition or symptoms.

Clang association is the term used to describe the use of rhymes and puns to link the rapid expression of disordered thoughts and ideas. It is sometimes seen in mania or schizophrenia where the person has a significant thought disorder.

Clinical depression is the term commonly used to make a distinction between a diagnosable (clinical) mood disorder and the more commonly experienced but non-illness-based lowering of mood that is a normal part of emotional experience. Clinical depression can be used as an umbrella term for the spectrum of clinically diagnosable depressive disorders.

A **clinical psychologist** is a person who has gained qualifications and experience in the therapeutic use of psychological techniques and therapies to treat people with emotional, behavioural and psychological problems. Clinical psychologists are widely employed in the NHS. They differ from psychiatrists in that they do not use a medical 'disease'-based model to understand and treat psychological problems and do not prescribe medication. Clinical psychologists tend to operate on a referral basis, using individual and group work methods to deliver psychotherapy interventions based on cognitive, behavioural, psychoanalytical or other interpersonal theories.

Clozapine (Clozaril) is an antipsychotic medication used to treat people with schizophrenic illnesses that have been resistant to other antipsychotic medications. Clozapine has fewer extrapyramidal side-effects than other antipsychotic medications but has the major potentially serious side-effect of depleting white blood cell production (neutropenia). As a result people receiving clozapine need to have regular blood tests to check their white cell levels.

Cognitive therapy is a form of psychotherapy developed by Aaron T. Beck. It is based on working to change the ways in which people's thinking and cognitive processing of experience determine their mood and behaviour. Cognitive therapy was originally developed to help people with depression but is also widely used as an intervention approach to anxiety and phobias.

Cognitive behaviour(al) therapy (CBT) developed out of behaviour therapy. It involves working to remodel or modify an individual's behaviour and cognitive processes. Intervention techniques are aimed at modifying a person's beliefs as well as their behaviour in relation to issues or experiences that cause them distress. CBT is widely used within mental health services and has been shown to be an effective intervention for affective disorder as well as some features of psychosis.

Community care – see **Care in the community**.

A **community psychiatric nurse (CPN)** is a qualified and experienced registered nurse who works in the community with individuals experiencing acute mental illness or requiring support for enduring mental health problems. CPNs usually work as part of a multi-disciplinary team and may be trained and qualified to provide specialist forms of psychotherapy for clients.

Complimentary therapy is an umbrella term for the various non-medical systems and approaches to healing and therapy. Complimentary therapies used in mental health settings include hypnosis, homeopathy, reflexology and acupuncture.

Compulsory admission to a place of safety is a phrase that is sometimes used by police officers, social workers and medical practitioners to describe the admission to hospital and detention under section of an individual who is, or is likely to be, a risk to themselves or others.

Confusion/a confusional state involves a disturbance in the individual's orientation to time, place or person. Confusion is sometimes accompanied by a reduction in level of consciousness, such as when the individual has a brain injury or is under the influence of alcohol or sedative drugs. People with a dementia-based illness may experience confusion without any reduction in their level of consciousness.

Counselling is an umbrella term used to describe a process of consultation and discussion where one individual (the counsellor) listens to another (the client) and offers support, guidance and sometimes advice or problem-solving suggestions to enable the client to address or resolve the difficulties that they face. The emphasis in counselling is on the client finding their own solution to their difficulties.

A **counsellor** is a person who is providing a counselling service (see above).

Crisis intervention is an intervention approach, used in psychotherapy and by a range of health professionals, that attempts to understand and intervene in episodes of acute crisis (evidenced by overdose, attempted suicide, deliberate self-harm) which people find it impossible or extremely difficult to deal with.

Cross-cultural psychiatry examines how concepts of health and illness, their underlying causes and the symptoms of mental illness are culturally determined. Diagnoses and judgements about what is 'normal' and 'abnormal' behaviour and emotion contain cultural assumptions of which indigenous members of a society are frequently unaware.

Cyclothymia/cyclothymic mood disorder involves cyclical mood swings. These are less severe and persistent than the mood swings characteristic of manic depressive psychosis. Cyclothymic disorder is only diagnosed where there has been disruption in the person's affect over an extended period.

Decompensate is a term used to indicate that a person has failed to use or apply protective and adaptive defence mechanisms when faced with a difficult or stressful situation. As a result, their non-coping is exacerbated.

De-escalation of aggression is used to describe any process of reducing the level of a person's expressed aggression. It is typically used to describe verbal methods of calming individuals whose rising levels of aggression are likely to lead to them becoming physically violent.

Deliberate self-harm (DSH) is an umbrella term describing any form of self-injury, typically being associated with cutting, overdoses or other consciously chosen and personally inflicted physical self-injury.

A **delusion** is a false personal belief that is out of keeping with a person's social or cultural background and maintained despite evidence or argument to the contrary. Delusions/delusional states are often features of schizophrenia, manic depression and dementia-based illnesses.

Dementia is a global, chronic organic impairment of mental functioning that occurs without any reduction in level of consciousness. Dementia-based illnesses are marked by changes in memory, personality, self-care ability, judgement, orientation and thinking ability (see Chapter 2.8, pp. 91–103).

Denial is a defence mechanism in which the person disavows thoughts, feelings, wishes or needs that, for some reason, cause them anxiety and that cannot, consciously, be addressed or dealt with.

Depersonalize/depersonalization are used to refer to the loss of a sense of self or identity or some personal reality. The person may complain of experiencing life as 'unreal' and of feeling 'strange'.

Depot injection/medication refer to anti-psychotic medication that is given via intramuscular injection. Depot medication is typically slow acting over a relatively long period of time.

Depression is a general term used to indicate a relatively mild down swing in mood. In clinical terms it is used to a identify relatively severe and persistent lowering of mood that is accompanied by emotional distress as well as physical, social and occupational dysfunction (see Section 2.3, pp. 34–47).

Disordered thinking is an umbrella term used to describe one or more problems in the content, flow or organization of thought processes.

Disorientation is a lack of awareness of time, place or person. This can be caused by substance misuse, neurological or organic brain disorder, high levels of anxiety or psychotic thought disorder.

Displacement activity involves the substitution or performance of one less stressful activity or behaviour for another more stressful, anxiety-provoking one.

Distorted body image is a feature of eating disorders, usually being associated with a person believing that they are 'fat' or larger than they actually are in objective terms.

Diversional activity is any activity that provides a stimulus to distract a person from some inappropriate or maladaptive preoccupation.

DSM is an acronym for the *Diagnostic and Statistical Manual of Mental Disorders* produced by the American Psychiatric Association.

Dysthymic refers to a generally depressed or low mood.

Dystonia is a postural disorder caused by damage to or disease in the basal ganglia in the brain. Signs include spasms in the shoulder, neck, trunk and limb muscles and the head being drawn back and held to one side. Acute dystonic reactions can be a side-effect of the extended or excessive use of psychotropic medication. Dystonic reactions can be relieved by anti-parkinsonian drugs such as procyclidine.

Early morning wakening (EMW) is a feature of depressive disorder. Patients usually complain about a pattern of waking (and not being able to get back to sleep), for no apparent reason, a few hours before they normally would.

Eating disorder is a diagnostic category that includes conditions such as anorexia nervosa, bulimia nervosa and overeating.

An **educational psychologist** is a teacher who has undertaken specialist psychology training and gained a formal qualification to practise in this area. Educational psychologists make assessments of the educational needs of children who may have special emotional, behavioural or learning needs.

Electro-convulsive therapy (ECT) is a physical treatment for severe depression. It involves a doctor using specialist equipment to pass a low voltage electrical current across the brain of a sedated patient. Patients receiving ECT may experience drowsiness, confusion and short-term memory loss immediately afterwards. Research suggests that ECT is an effective treatment for relatively intractable severe depression thought the precise reason for this is unclear.

Emotionally labile simply means 'emotionally changeable'. The term is typically used when a person appears to have apparently spontaneous 'outbursts' of distress that they are unable to control.

Endogenous depression is an 'old' term that is used to refer to depressive disorder that has an apparently 'internal' (physical or psychological) cause. It was contrasted with *reactive depression*, which could be explained by reference to identifiable 'external' causes.

Euthymic mood is a term used to describe a normal mood state. This follows a pattern of relatively minor fluctuations that are appropriate responses to the situation or events that occur.

Expressed emotion (EE) is a term used to describe the degree of warmth or hostility in a relationship. It is assessed where one person is talking about their relationship with another. High expressed emotion (HEE) involves high levels of criticism and hostility and is known to have a negative effect on the mental state and prognosis of individuals in the family who experience mental health problems.

Extra-pyramidal side-effects (EPS) result from taking some antipsychotic drugs, particularly phenothiazines, which work by blocking certain dopamine receptors in the extra-pyramidal tract of the brain and thus give rise to extra-pyramidal symptoms. These include **tardive dyskinesia**, **akathisia**, **dystonia** and **Parkinsonian** symptoms. Careful dose management and the additional use of procyclidine can be used to reduce these side-effects.

Factitious disorder is an umbrella term used to describe psychological or other symptoms of psychiatric disorder that are voluntarily produced that are feigned and simulated for some unspoken purpose.

Family therapy is an umbrella term used to describe forms of psychotherapeutic group work where a family is treated as a whole unit rather than as independent individuals requiring personal, individual therapy. There are various forms and models of family therapy/family work, though all involve one or more family therapists taking on a group facilitator/therapist role in sessions with the whole family group.

First rank symptoms is an 'old' term associated with schizophrenia. It was first used by Kurt Schneider, a German psychiatrist, to identify those symptoms that he thought were diagnostic or definitive of schizophrenia. These include thought disorder, feelings of passivity and auditory hallucinations in the third person. The term tends not to be used diagnostically by psychiatrists or other mental health specialists anymore but can be found in some patient's notes or in older literature on schizophrenia.

Flight of ideas is a feature of thought disorder where the person experiences, and often expresses, a fast continuous but fragmentary stream of ideas, thoughts and images. This stream of ideas does not appear to have a logical or coherent organising pattern. It is most commonly observed where the individual is experiencing the manic phase of a bipolar illness or in mania itself.

Florid symptoms are active, overtly expressed and vivid changes in behaviour or other expressions of clear mental disorder. The term is often used to describe a person's experience of hallucinations or thought disorder.

Forensic psychiatry focuses on the overlaps between mental disorder, offending behaviour and legal issues. A **Forensic assessment** is usually made by specialist forensic psychiatry staff for the purpose of establishing the extent to which a person's mental health problems may involve or lead to dangerous behaviour and is fundamentally driven by 'risk' assessment.

Formal thought disorder is the term used to indicate that the signs and symptoms that a person presents with fit a general pattern or specific rules/criteria (ICD, for example) to the extent that they are diagnostic of thought disorder. The term is usually applied to problems with the form or structure of thinking rather than the content of the person's thoughts.

Free floating anxiety is a form of pervasive and unfocused anxiety. The term is often used synonymously with generalized anxiety disorder.

Freudian refers to any approach or theory that fits or follows the theories and concepts developed by Sigmund Freud. The term is used when there is some primary focus or reference to the role of unconscious processes as motivators of behaviour or a preference for making deep interpretations by reference to early experiences or 'hidden' layers of the psyche.

Functional disorder is an umbrella term used to indicate that the cause of the disorder is unknown in the sense that there is no observable organic pathology. Functional psychoses include schizophrenia and bipolar disorder.

Galactorrhoea is abnormal, copious milk secretion.

Generalized anxiety disorder is a state of inappropriate, severe anxiety that appears to have no adequate cause (see Section 2.4, p. 49).

GPI is an acronym for 'general paralysis of the insane'. This alarming term refers to the later consequences of syphillis infection (cerebrosyphilis) which are now very rarely seen. As the name suggests, the key (ultimate) symptom was physical paralysis, preceded by spastic weakness of the limbs and the general symptoms associated with dementia.

Grandiose delusions are beliefs that a person has an exalted wealth, status and/or special powers/abilities. These can be a symptom of bipolar disorder, mania or schizophrenia.

Group therapy is a general term that describes the psychotherapeutic use of groups working with a group leader or facilitator. The interactions and relationships within the group are used as part of the therapeutic process, with the facilitator observing and managing the group dynamics. Groups are felt to be an effective way of sharing problems, providing emotional support and an environment for trying out new ways of relating to people.

Gynaecomastia is the development of breasts in a male. This can be a severe side-effect of the overuse of psychotropic medication.

An **hallucination** is a sensory impression that is experienced as 'real' despite there being no external environmental stimuli to trigger it. Hallucinations can be auditory, visual, tactile, olfactory (smell) or gustatory (taste). They are a characteristic symptom of schizophrenia, though they can also be experienced as a result of severe exhaustion, drug or alcohol use, in dementia or as a result of a brain injury.

Hebephrenic schizophrenia/hebephrenia is an old, outdated term used to describe a form of schizophrenia characterized by florid thought disorder and emotional incongruity, such as inappropriate outbursts of giggling or laughing. Bizarre hypochondriacal delusions, auditory hallucinations and odd mannerisms were also felt to be common features of hebephrenia.

Huntington's chorea/disease is an inherited condition that tends to appear in half of the children of parents who carry the defective gene as a dominant characteristic. Symptoms, beginning in early middle age (30s), include **choroid** and **athetoid** movements that initially affect the face and limbs but spread to the whole body, as well as behaviour and personality changes. The disease is degenerative over a period of 10–20 years and with brain degeneration leading to death (see 'A–Z of support groups').

Hypomania is the term used to describe a relatively mild degree of mania. Elated mood tends to lead to a reduction in ability to make appropriate judgements and a failure to observe normal social restraints on behaviour. The person appears excitable with rapid speech and a lot of energy. They can become irritable quite easily. The person does not appear as elated as in hypermania.

ICD is an acronym for the *International Classification of Diseases.*

Ideas of reference are beliefs that casual remarks or actions have a special significance. They are held with less conviction than delusions. For example, television broadcasts are felt by individuals to refer to them in particular.

Incongruous emotions/affect are emotions or an affect that are out of keeping with or inappropriate to the circumstances in which they are expressed.

Jungian refers to the model of thinking or therapeutic approach of Carl Gustav Jung. Jung developed an analytical psychology and therapeutic approach that sees 'natural energy' flowing between 'opposites' and a striving for self-realization.

Kemadrin is another (old) term for procyclidine. It is sometimes used by people who have chronic mental health problems or may be seen in old notes.

Key worker is a term that is used generally to refer to the care professional (social worker, nurse or psychiatrist) or support worker who has overall, co-ordinating responsibility for an individual's care. The term is used specifically in **Care Programme Approach** documents to identify the professional who undertakes this role and oversees the implementation of the individuals care plan.

Knight's move thinking is a form of thought disorder that is characteristic of schizophrenia. It involves the person apparently jumping from one idea to another without there being any apparent connection between the ideas. The association between ideas appears bizarre and illogical. The 'knight's move' is a metaphorical reference to chess where the knight is the only piece allowed to move erratically by jumping over other pieces.

Labile/lability – see **emotional lability** above.

Lanugo is the fine, downy hair that develops on the extremities and trunk of people who are substantially underweight as a consequence of anorexia nervosa. It is also a natural feature covering the body of the fetus and the premature infant.

Lithium is a drug that is commonly used in the treatment of manic depression to stabilize mood fluctuations. It has a narrow therapeutic range so levels in the body have to be checked through regular blood tests. Toxic levels can lead to encephalopathy and death.

'Lloyd George notes' refer to the paper record system kept by most GPs. Increasingly, these are being replaced by computer-held records.

Maintenance medication/doses are terms used to describe repeat prescriptions or established doses, of drugs that a person receives on a regular or ongoing basis to maintain their mental state.

Major tranquillizer is an old, and now outdated, term used to describe antipsychotic/neuroleptic drugs. The term is outdated because the key therapeutic value is the antipsychotic rather than the tranquillizing property.

Mania is a disordered mental state in which the individual experiences extreme excitement and physical over-activity or extravagant behaviour. The person's mood is usually elated or euphoric, though they can also be very irritable, and their speech can be rapid and thoughts apparently disorganized. 'Manic' is a term used to indicate that the person is experiencing mania.

Manic depression is another term for bipolar disorder (see Section 2.2, pp. 25–33).

Melancholia is a general, non-clinical term used to describe a state of extreme or deep depression in which the person has a sense of foreboding and a general insensitivity to stimulation.

Mental state simply means state of mind. The **mental state examination** (MSE) is a formal way of assessing mental state that is used by psychiatrists and other medical practitioners.

Minor tranquillizer is an 'old' term used to describe anxiolytic medication such as lorazepam and diazepam.

MIND is a national registered charity working with an on behalf of people with mental health problems. More information and contact details are provided in 'A–Z of support groups'.

The Mental Health Act (1983) is the key piece of legislation that expresses the law in relation to the rights and treatment of people with mental illnesses who are detained in hospital in England, Wales and Northern Ireland. **The Mental Health (Scotland) Act 1984** performs the same function in Scotland and contains slightly different provisions and procedures.

Modified narcosis is an old, and probably now rarely used, detoxification treatment for people with drug misuse problems. It involved the use of sedative drugs to put the person into a state of unconsciousness for relatively long periods of time (days) while their body was detoxified, and the person withdrew, from the drugs they misused.

Music therapy involves the use of music as a therapeutic medium to facilitate emotional release and relaxation.

Narcosis is a state of unconsciousness produced by a narcotic drug (see also **modified narcosis**).

National Schizophrenia Fellowship is a voluntary sector organization that works with and on behalf of people (sufferers and their families) who experience the impact of severe mental health problems such as schizophrenia (see 'A–Z of groups').

Negative symptoms is a term used to describe features of psychoses, such as chronic schizophrenia involving lethargy, lack of motivation, flat affect, thought blocking and social withdrawal.

Neologisms are new words or phrases, or new meanings attached to existing words or phrases. These tend to have meaning to the speaker but not to the listener, for example, describing a feeling called 'sprinkle' in the arm. Neologisms are a feature of thought disorder.

Neuroleptic medications are drugs that act on the nervous system.

Neuroleptic malignancy syndrome is a serious side-effect of the overuse of antipsychotic medication. Key signs and symptoms include high fever, severe muscular rigidity, confusion and apparent lowering of consciousness and can lead to death. Neuroleptic medication must be stopped immediately and the situation treated as a medical emergency.

Neurolinguistic programming (NLP) is a set of techniques that are used to influence and modify behaviour and beliefs. It is based on assumed relations between linguistic forms, memory and behaviour.

Neurosis is an umbrella term used to describe forms of mental disorder in which normal emotional responses or behaviours are distorted or exaggerated, contact with reality is retained and the sufferer recognizes their symptoms as being 'abnormal'.

Neurotransmitter is a naturally occurring biochemical substance, such as dopamine and noradrenaline that is released from nerve endings to produce activity in other nerves.

An **occupational therapist** is a health professional who uses selected activities to promote optimal functioning within daily life. OTs work with people experiencing a broad range of disabling conditions (physical and mental), using creative activity, group work, educational and other supportive activities that are most appropriate and relevant to the individual to enable them to develop and maintain their occupational performance.

Oculargyrocrisis is an acute reaction to psychotropic medication. It begins with the person developing a fixed stare before their eyes rotate upwards, then to the side and remain fixed in that position. This is very alarming and distressing for the person. The symptoms are relieved by procyclidine or other anti-Parkinsonian agents usually given by intramuscular injection.

Organic psychosis refers to a psychotic disorder that has a clear, identifiable physical cause. This is usually a brain injury or disorder.

A **panic attack** is a short but distressing episode of intense anxiety (see Section 2.4, pp. 48–56).

Paranoia is a mental disorder that is characterized by persecutory delusions, jealousy or delusions of grandeur and the absence of other psychotic symptoms such as hallucinations. It is relatively rare, though it tends to be a chronic problem.

Paranoid schizophrenia is a form of schizophrenia (see Section 2.1, pp. 13–24) characterized by prominent persecutory delusions, which co-exist with other symptoms of psychosis such as hallucinations and passivity phenomena.

Paraphrenia is a mental disorder first occurring in later life that is often presented by elderly deaf people. It is characterized by systematic paranoid delusions and prominent hallucinations and the absence of any other psychotic symptoms in which there is loss of contact with reality.

Parasuicide is another term for acts deliberate self-harm where there is no apparent or expressed wish to die.

Passivity experience/phenomena are a characteristic feature of psychosis. They are delusional beliefs that the person is being affected or controlled by an external force or person. Passivity phenomena include thought insertion, 'made actions', 'made feelings' and somatic passivity.

Persecutory delusions are a feature of some people's experience of psychosis. They are also referred to as **paranoid delusions** and involve the person believing with strong conviction that they are the victim of a plot or conspiracy to harm them or their interests.

Personality disorder is an umbrella term used to describe any deeply ingrained and maladaptive pattern of behaviour or way of relating to others. It is now used to identify disorders that are neither neuroses or psychoses, in which the individual's overall personality and behaviour is marked by pathological development and expression with relatively little anxiety or distress.

Peurperal psychosis is also known as **post-natal psychosis**. It is a psychotic mental disorder that has a strong affective presentation, though there is some debate about whether it is a condition that is peculiar to childbirth or whether it arises from causes that are unrelated to the childbirth itself.

Phenothiazines are a group of drugs used to treat mental disorder. The classic phenothiazine medication is chlorpromazine.

Phobia is a form of specific, focused anxiety (see Section 2.4, pp. 48–56).

Phototoxicity is a sensitivity to sunlight – where even the slightest exposure can cause severe sunburn – and it is an unwanted side-effect of phenothiazines such as chlorpromazine.

Polydipsia is an abnormal thirst that leads to the ingestion of large amounts of fluid. It is a symptom of diabetes but is also a relatively rare psychological disorder. It can prove fatal of sodium levels in the blood are severely reduced so that convulsions, coma and death occur.

Positive symptoms is a term that is sometimes used to refer to florid or acute symptoms of mental disorder.

Post-natal depression is a form of relatively severe and depressive disorder that can occur following childbirth (see Section 2.3, pp. 34–47).

Post-traumatic stress disorder (PTSD) is an anxiety-based disorder that results from experiences of major, traumatic personal stress such as sexual assault or exposure to warfare. The stress reaction can be delayed with the sufferers experiencing persistent, recurrent memories or 'flashbacks' of the event together with isolation, guilt, and poor concentration. PTSD can lead to depressive disorder.

Pre-morbid personality is a term used to refer to the pattern or state of the person's personality before the onset of their mental health problems.

Prodromal relates to the period of time between the appearance of the first symptoms and the development of the full disorder. It is generally used to describe the process of an infectious disease but is sometimes used by medical staff to describe the process of any disorder.

Projection is a defence mechanism in which the individual attributes their own motives, feelings or qualities to others. This is usually done because the person cannot tolerate the high levels of anxiety that are provoked by the motives or feelings involved.

Protocols are formal documents that set out the procedures to be followed in the event of a given situation arising, for example, an aggressive incident, or with regard to the specific treatment of a condition or disorder. They are usually developed at a local level and take into account all professionals who will be involved and specify the role of each.

A **psychodynamic approach** to psychotherapy or assessment of mental disorder is one that uses the main concepts of psychoanalysis. The psychodynamic approach views the adult personality as a product of child development and mental health problems as having their roots in early relationships and experiences.

Psychometric tests are used to measure various forms of psychological experience, ability or aptitude. They provide a score that relates to a scale of severity. This has been developed using statistical principles, which provide an average score in the general population against which to compare.

Psychomotor retardation is a term applied to disorders where muscular activity is reduced as a result of cerebral disturbance. It can be a feature of severe depressive disorder and schizophrenia, for example.

Psychopath(y) is a mental disorder that is neither a psychosis or a neurosis and is a form of personality disorder. People with a psychopathic personality disorder typically engage in anti-social behaviour for which they feel little or no guilt or remorse. Additionally they tend to have difficulty in forming and maintaining effective emotional relationships with others.

Psychosexual disorder is an umbrella term used to refer to sexual problems that have a significant mental component.

Psychotic depression is an 'old' term that is sometimes used to describe forms of severe depressive disorder where delusions and feelings of hopelessness and worthlessness result in some loss of contact with reality. The term is sometimes used synonymously with **endogenous depression**.

Psychotropic medication is an umbrella term used to describe the broad range of mood altering drugs. These include antidepressants, sedatives, and tranquillizers.

Psychoses/psychotic disorders are those conditions, such as schizophrenia and manic depression/bipolar disorder, where the person experiences a disturbed mental state that involve a loss of contact with reality, into which the person has little insight. Psychoses distort the personality and involve the construction of a false, subjective environment in the form of delusions, hallucinations and thought disorder.

A **psychotherapist** is a person who practices one of the many forms of psychotherapy. Client-centred, family and cognitive behavioural therapy are forms of psychotherapy that are relatively widely known and practised in NHS mental health services.

Rapid cycling is a term used to refer to the occurrence of four or more affective episodes (of mania or depression) in a year. Rapid cycling is a feature of bipolar disorder or manic depression.

Rationalization is a defence mechanism used to 'save face' by explaining logically erratic, unacceptable or embarrassing feelings or behaviour.

Rational emotive therapy is a form of psychotherapy developed by Albert Ellis. It focuses on rational, problem-solving aspects of emotional and behavioural problems. It is similar to cognitive therapy but is more therapist-directed with the therapist telling the client what they must do to resolve their problems and encouraging them to address them.

Reactive depression is an 'old' but still commonly used term that describes forms of depressive disorder that have a clear, identifiable and understandable trigger factor(s). It tends to be contrasted with endogenous depression.

Reality orientation is a method of responding to the disorientation of people with dementia and other states of confusion. It uses verbal and visual cues to remind the person where they are and why they are there, stimulating them to stay in the 'here-and-now'.

Registered mental nurses (RMN) are trained and qualified specialist nurses who work with people experiencing acute and chronic mental disorders in a variety of in-patient, out-patient and community settings. RMNs have often undertaken further training in specialist forms of counselling, psychotherapy or behavioural intervention.

Relapse/relapse rate refers to the general failure or falling back of progress in achieving a healthy mental state.

Reminiscence therapy is a widely used form of supportive psychotherapy in settings where older people with mental health problems are cared for. It involves the use of memory prompt materials and techniques to aid the recall of information about, and emotions associated with earlier life experiences and life history. The goals of reminiscence therapy are usually to resolve tensions, guilt and anxiety.

Retrocollis describes muscle spasm, which forces the head and neck back. This occurs during an **oculargyric crisis**.

SANE is a voluntary sector organization that provides support and information on a wide range of mental health problems (see 'A–Z of support groups', pp. 134–154).

Schizo-affective disorder straddles the two separate diagnoses of schizophrenia and bi-polar affective disorder. It is episodic in nature and simultaneously combines either of the extremes of affect (mood) – mania or depression – with symptoms of schizophrenia. The treatment usually involves anti-psychotic medication, including maintenance depot doses, and may well include medication typically used in bi-polar affective disorder. The prognosis is better than that for schizophrenia.

Schizophrenia is a psychotic disorder characterised by hallucinations and delusional beliefs (see Section 2.1, pp. 13–24).

Seasonal affective disorder (SAD) is a recurrent affective disorder that occurs during the autumn and winter months. It is thought to be related to physiological changes that result from the reduction in day light during these periods.

'Sectioned' is a term used to refer to the compulsory admission and detention in hospital of an individual under the legal provisions of the Mental Health Act (1983) or the Mental Health (Scotland) Act (1984).

Self-help groups are user-led, support and therapy groups. They are usually organized and supported by national voluntary groups, such as MIND or Alcoholics Anonymous, but are also sometimes developed and facilitated by statutory sector staff.

Simple schizophrenia is an old, outmoded term that is sometimes used to describe a form of schizophrenia that is characterized by odd and eccentric behaviour, apathy/indifference and a lack of positive emotional expression, poor social skills and a tendency to drift onto the fringes of society.

Split personality is an outmoded and wrong description of the consequences of schizophrenia. People with schizophrenic illnesses have only one personality though this may be affected by the illness.

SSRI is an acronym for selective serotonin re-uptake inhibitor. This is a form of anti-depressant medication.

Stress is a very widely used term to describe states of psychological tension that are produced by, or are the outcome of, social and psychological forces and pressures.

Substance abuse/misuse is an umbrella term that is used to classify various forms of non-medical use of alcohol, drugs (prescribed, medicinal and non-prescribed non-medicinal) and other stimulants to affect physical and psychological functioning.

Suicide is the intentional act of taking one's life. The intention to die distinguishes it from *parasuicide*. *Suicidal thoughts* are a feature of severe depressive disorders but do not always lead to suicidal acts.

The Supervision Register was a feature of the aftercare arrangements of the **care programme approach**. People with mental health problems that required admission and treatment in hospital under the Mental Health Act were placed on the supervision register if their mental disorder led to offending behaviour or was felt to result in risks to themselves or others.

Tardive dyskinesia (TD) is a chronic movement disorder that is characterised by choroid and athetoid movements. It is associated with the long-term use of neuroleptic medication.

Thought block is a symptom of psychotic disorder, particularly schizophrenia, though it may also occur in severe depressive disorder. It is the sudden interruption of a train of thought so that the person experiences a 'blank' and cannot then recall what they were talking or thinking about.

Thought broadcast is a delusional belief that one's thoughts can be read/heard by others or transmitted to other people in some way. It is a symptom of some forms of schizophrenia.

Thought disorder is an umbrella term used to describe any disorder in thinking. See also formal thought disorder. Features of thought disorder include delusions, flight of ideas and ideas of reference.

Thought insertion is a term used to describe the delusional belief that thoughts are being inserted into one's head by an external agency. It is a 'passivity' symptom of schizophrenia and may be described in a similar way to auditory hallucinations but the thoughts are not heard as 'external' in the way that 'voices' are.

Thought withdrawal is a term used to describe the delusional belief that one's thoughts are being removed by an external agency. Again, it is a relatively common symptom of schizophrenia.

Torticollis is a turning movement of the head that occurs persistently with the outcome being that the person holds their head continuously to one side. The spasm of the neck muscles is often painful. Torticollis is a potential side-effect of the prolonged use of some neuroleptic medications and is also a feature of an **oculargyric crisis**.

Tourette's syndrome is a relatively rare neurological syndrome characterized by severe and multiple tic movements, grunting sounds and involuntary obscene speech. The condition usually has its onset in childhood and becomes chronic.

Transactional analysis is a form of psychotherapy developed by Eric Berne. It focuses on ego states and relating in appropriate, mature and adaptive ways.

Uni-polar affective disorder refers to the incidence of either depression or mania as a mood problem and is contrasted with bi-polar disorder where the person experiences problematic episodes of both elevated and lowered mood.

Validation therapy was developed as a way of communicating with people with dementia. It attempts to relate to the person's feelings by validating and supporting what they say – even if this does not apparently correspond with reality – because it has meaning for them. It is not collusion, but rather an acknowledgement that this is their reality and is therefore valid.

Voluntary agencies are non-government organizations that are, typically, also registered charities. There are many examples in the mental health field, including **MIND, National Schizophrenia Fellowship** and the **Eating Disorders Association** (see 'A–Z of support groups'). They tend to provide support/advice, information and self help services, though in some cases they also provide direct care services as an alternative to those offered by statutory mental health service providers.

Waxy flexibility is a sign of catatonia. The person's limbs are held indefinitely in the position in which they are placed as though they have been moulded out of wax. This is also sometimes referred to as wavy flexibility.

Word salad is a symptom of psychosis, typically schizophrenia. The person utters speech that is a bizarre, incoherent and apparently nonsensical mix ('salad') of disconnected and unrelated words and phrases.

The Z-tracking technique is a way of giving a depot or intra-muscular injection (see Section 3.2, pp. 127–133).

INDEX